Dream Fish and Road Trips

Books by E. Donnall Thomas Jr.

Whitefish Can't Jump
Fool Hen Blues
Longbows in the Far North
Longbow Country
Dream Fish and Road Trips

Dream Fish and Road Trips

Alaska, Montana, and Beyond

E. Donnall Thomas Jr.

Lyons & Burford, Publishers

Printed in the United States of America

10   9   8   7   6   5   4   3   2   1

Illustrations by David Wharton
Design by The BookSetters Co.

Library of Congress Cataloging-in-Publication Data

Thomas, E. Donnall.
   Dream fish and road trips : Alaska, Montana, and beyond / E. Donnall Thomas, Jr.
       p.   cm.
   ISBN 1-55821-429-1 (cloth)
   1. Fly fishing. 2. Fly fishing—Alaska. 3. Fly fishing—Montana.
I. Title.
SH456.T486   1996
799.1'2—dc20   95-33445
                                                                    CIP

To Deirdre

Table of Contents

Acknowledgments

I would like to express my thanks to Lori Thomas and Janet Grensten for their help with the preparation of this manuscript, and to Jim Babb for his usual precise editing.

In different form, some of the material in this book has appeared in print previously, in *Alaska, Gray's Sporting Journal, Fly Rod and Reel, Sporting Classics, Game Journal,* and *Shimano Fishing.* I appreciate the opportunity to rework these pieces for inclusion in this volume.

"Everything good is on the highway."
—*Ralph Waldo Emerson*

Part I

ALASKA

The thing I miss most is the light.

We usually take light for granted, as an elusive physical entity that rises in the morning, fades in the evening, and illuminates our triumphs and failures in between. It's difficult to realize just how ordinary most light is until you enjoy it in one of its extraordinary forms, and Alaska's is the most extraordinary light I have ever experienced.

There are simple physical explanations for the unique character of arctic light. The sun is always off to the south, which means that it's never far from the horizon whether you're seeing a lot of it in the summer or almost none of it in the winter. Its rays are filtered by layers of atmosphere, which soften and deprive the light of its edges. Coupled with the rugged terrain, the effect is to make the landscape glow, even at night when the sun lies just around the corner of the world.

Alaska's light is at its best, however, when you're not even aware of its presence, let alone the scientific explanations for its magic. At times it just sneaks up on you and makes you stop doing whatever you are doing until you finally realize why you are staring at a mountain or a river that you have seen a hundred times before. Light like this can suffuse ordinary scenes, casting a spell over rocks and trees and water to create a theater of its own where all the rules are different and absolutely nothing is ordinary.

What a place to go fishing.

Alaska, of course, is really more of a subcontinent than a state, and it seems a little silly to lump it in with such geographic entities as Connecticut and North Dakota. I recognized as much long ago when, as a college student, I kept a map of Alaska on my wall right through all the sixties craziness to remind me that there really were wild places left in the world. I sensed that Alaska was too big just to visit, and I was right. When I finally got around to going I stayed for six years. Its size turned out to be one of my few preconceptions that proved accurate.

Alaska is riddled with all sorts of paradoxes ranging from cultural to social to economic, but since the subject of this book is fish, it seems appropriate to let fish illustrate the point. Despite its deserved reputation as home to some of the world's greatest fishing, Alaska is also home to some of the world's leanest fish habitat. This may be a hard concept to grasp when schools of salmon are teeming all around you, but most of Alaska's fresh water turns out to be nearly sterile. The ultimate source of all that bounty is the sea, and virtually all Alaska gamefish have links to salt water, whether directly, in the case of anadromous fish, or indirectly, in the case of other species that depend on salmon to prime the food chain's pump with protein and calories from eggs, smolt, and decaying bodies.

For an area as vast as Alaska proves to be when you set out to explore it, places to fish (at least the good ones) are surprisingly few and far between. Those accessible from Alaska's limited road system are so crowded they're almost impossible to enjoy fishing unless you're also engaged in a parallel study of human behavioral pathology. Those not readily accessible often obligate the visitor to deal with bears, mosquitoes, foul weather, bush flying, brush, giardiasis, and general despair. Soon after my own arrival in the Great Land, I reconciled these facts by learning to ignore what went on along the roads and to love the challenges of the bush. To avoid disappointment, I suggest that others of like mind learn to do the same.

Finally, I note with irony that while Alaska is certainly home to some of the world's best outdoor sport, it is also home to some of the world's strangest standards of the outdoor sporting ethic. A curious social phenomenon that I observed over and over during my residence in the state—the compulsive urge to snag, net, beat, club, and kill fish by the boatload—seems to transcend all demographic boundaries. This is not the sniffling protest of a mortified, politically correct fly fisher. I take pride in distancing myself from such affected sentiment by dispatching a fish for dinner whenever it is biologically appropriate. But put a bunch of salmon in an accessible Alaska stream and open a personal-use dipnet fishery and you will see civilized people behave as civilized people have not behaved since the days of the Roman Coliseum.

I comment on these tendencies not so much in the interest of condemnation as in the interest of understanding. Perhaps they're an expression of some residual Frontier Effect, an insatiable urge to plunder when released from the constraints of urban habit. Perhaps they simply reflect frustration with those paradoxes outlined earlier, resulting in the notion that if one has done what one has to do in order to get (finally) where the fish are, then one should by-God get while the getting is good. Whatever the case, such gluttonous frenzies should remind us of what happened to the buffalo and the passenger pigeon and the Michigan grayling, a realization of little value unless we come to terms with the same impulses lurking within our own hearts.

All this may sound like a strange way to introduce a series of essays devoted to the romantic proposition that Alaska is one of the greatest places on earth to spend time outdoors with a fly rod in your hand, but I've always preferred my Alaska straight up, warts and all. Its contradictions only heighten the appreciation of what is truly Great about the Great Land.

And there is plenty of Great for everyone, including those who define the outdoors with fly rods. From the steelhead streams of the southeastern panhandle to the salmon runs of Cook Inlet and Bristol Bay to the lonely arctic haunts of sheefish, grayling, and char, there is more fishing to be done in Alaska than anyone could do in a lifetime. Indeed, it is the overwhelming sense of possibilities that draws many of us back again and again.

Once you manage to arrive in the right place at the right time (not always an easy task, as it turns out), fly fishing Alaska waters is seldom a highly technical affair, at least compared with the dithering over entomology and fly selection common to more refined settings. Most of the challenge is in getting there; once you start casting, tenacity becomes more important than technique. Of course there are exceptions to this principle (matching salmon eggs can sometimes be as tedious as matching mayflies), but those who cannot imagine catching fish without reciting the Latin names of insects usually have some major attitude adjustment in store when they head north for the first time.

Personally, I have no problem with the in-your-face aspects of Alaska fly fishing, because the absence of technical demands frees me to keep my attention focused outside my fly book where it belongs. For above all else, Alaska is the land of the Big Show, where nature is always on display. Whatever Alaska fishing lacks in subtlety, it more than makes up for in natural spectacle. Anyone who fails to be moved at a primal level by the sight of vast schools of salmon fighting their way upstream in response to inscrutable instincts to procreate and die probably shouldn't be there in the first place.

That's what keeps me thinking about Alaska even now, nearly ten years after my departure. There is just no escaping the sense that the decision to live anywhere else on earth is a compromise, that by choosing to do so I have yielded to the weak instincts of convenience and creature comfort. And I have.

But there was so much to take away with me, and at no cost to anyone or anything. Those are the memories that remain: rainbows that glow like pink neon signs, grayling displaying outlandish dorsal fins, kings charging downriver on the end of a line with the determination of dangerous game, steelhead that made tiny nameless streams come alive just for me.

Sometimes when the sun is low and the light is just right, I can see them still.

Chapter 1

Promises, Promises

 As the water flows, it is scarcely two miles from the outlet of Salmon Bay Lake to the tideline. Nonetheless, the river manages to provide everything an anadromous fish could ask for in its short length, from the gentle beds of pea gravel just below the lake to the riotous descent through the rain forest to the complex marine environment where fresh water transitions to salt. This is steelhead country, with clear water and ample rain and a vital carpet of conifers to keep everything from washing away forever into the sea. That's all the fish need, and since it's good enough for them, there's no reason why it shouldn't be good enough for us.

It is now early May, a bit late for Salmon Bay River steelhead according to conventional wisdom, but not according to my personal experience. We have been bowhunting bears here for three days now, and as you might imagine that's the sort of enterprise that occasionally demands a break. The bears are so big, the forests so deep. I am ready to put all that behind me for awhile, and my agenda for the afternoon calls for nothing more demanding than a leisurely stroll up the river with fly rod in hand.

In fact, the notion of a leisurely stroll anywhere in southeast Alaska is a bit of a stretch. By local standards the walk along Salmon Bay River is relatively benign, since there is a trail of sorts from the tideline to the lake's outlet that the Forest Service sort of maintains, the way the Forest

Service sort of does a lot of things here. At any rate, it's still one of the area's easier streamside hikes, but the fishing itself is another matter.

This afternoon we have walked up past the two tide pools just above the salt water. Ray stayed behind to work a favorite run in the river's middle reaches and I stand alone on a massive fallen log watching the river below dance away downstream. My instincts tell me that there are fish down there bound for the spawning grounds upstream. The technical aspects of the problem are simply stated: How do you get a fly to the fish without killing yourself?

I pace back and forth across the log like a bear, choosing my route down to the water with uneasy discretion. No matter. My final approach to streamside is a graceless affair, involving a handful of devil's club and a nifty carom off a large, jagged rock, but at least I'm in the right place when I stop rolling. The fly, however, is not, and it takes another five minutes of precarious maneuvering to get into casting position. There will be no complex greased-line techniques today, no elegant mends, no powerful double hauls. Salmon Bay River just isn't the proper venue for that sort of thing, no matter how much we might wish otherwise. All I want right now is to get the fly (something weighty and bright; the details scarcely matter) into the short, sweet lick of current over against the opposite bank. If a fish is in this riffle, that's where it'll be.

It costs me two flies, a bruised knee, and a wet left foot to prove that the little slot is empty, but I'm a philosopher when it comes to this sort of thing, as anyone who regularly fishes for Alaska steelhead eventually must become. My possibilities here exhausted, there is nothing left to do but fight my way upstream to the next potential holding water, a process I will repeat half a dozen times over the next hour or so.

Finally I find myself perched on a slippery rock between a monumental logjam downstream and a division in the river's channel above. I'm about out of water, except for the pea gravel section upstream where the fish will be spawning and where they have certainly earned the right to make more steelhead in peace. Nestled against the opposite bank, one last slot invites a fly, and it doesn't seem right to turn back without offering it one.

The fly hits the water, tumbles down, disappears. The line hesitates and I strike reflexively, fully prepared for the sharp, sterile tick of hook on rock followed by the unyielding disappointment of a snag. This time, however, the resistance is soft and vital, and at the hook's impact a yard-long section of streambed appears to detach itself from the bottom and hurtle upstream with a life of its own.

My first thought is, I've got him! My second thought is, He's got me! Here are the brutal facts. Attached by a flimsy section of tippet to a steelhead in the fifteen pound–plus range, I am balanced precariously on a rock upon which my continued presence was problematic even before the fish struck. The water is littered with snags in all directions, and twenty yards downstream the logjam offers the fish a definitive escape route. I may outweigh my quarry by a hundred seventy or so pounds, but my money is on the steelhead.

And it doesn't take long to confirm my abilities as a handicapper. The fish roars upstream through the riffle above its original lie, then back down again and past my rock, showing enough pink to confirm it's a male, then straight for the warren of downed logs. I have no strategy left but to apply progressively more ridiculous amounts of pressure, which I do, with the inevitable result.

The fish is gone. My line trails in the water like something dead; Salmon Bay River continues on to the sea, indifferent to the brief moment of high drama just played out upon its stage. Though the steelhead swims free, our encounter has given me a measure of freedom all my own. There has been a connection. The river made a promise and fulfilled it. The rest of the afternoon feels larger now, larger than even the trees and the sea can make it.

Wild fish can do that to you anytime you're willing to let them. It isn't necessary to catch them. It is only necessary that they be there.

The biologists assure us that the steelhead of southeast Alaska are the same as steelhead everywhere: *Oncorhynchus mykiss*, following a long taxonomic evolution that can be traced back to *Salmo irideus* in half a dozen different steps. Fishing for steelhead here, however, is quite unlike fishing for steelhead anywhere else.

As a species, the steelhead's character is virtually defined by the North Pacific, from which all *Oncorhynchus* evolved and to which each native steelhead must still return. It is possible to fish for them in places remote from that intimidating body of water, in the Snake River drainage, for example, or interior British Columbia, but the distance from the sea there is tangible, and somehow compromises the essence of the steelhead experience. No such detachment exists in southeast Alaska, where the ocean seems everywhere and the streams that hold the fish are short and eager as they hurry toward the sea. The inescapable influence of tides and salt water provides a greater sense of intimacy with the fish than inland waters, no matter how good the fishing.

The steelhead, like the caribou and grizzly, originated on the Old World side of the Pacific Rim. So did the area's first human inhabitants, who arrived by way of the land bridge across what is now the Bering Strait, and its first colonialists, members of the Russian-American Company who came by sea twenty thousand years later. There is no intrinsic reason why an appreciation of the steelhead's transpacific origins should enhance my enjoyment of its pursuit, but it does. Like the wolf and the wild sheep, the steelhead offers a biological reminder of Alaska's unique fusion of Old World and New. Those are easy matters to lose track of while fishing for steelhead in Idaho. Not so in southeast Alaska, where Russian place-names cover the map, brown bears wander the beaches, and the cold, gray Pacific is always waiting just downstream no matter where you are.

And then there's the rain, without which no discussion of southeast Alaska can be complete. While I can remember catching steelhead under clear skies in other places, those experiences felt disjointed somehow, as if some essential ingredient were missing. Rain is trophic to steelhead in a fundamental way that makes wet weather central to their enjoyment, for it is rain that coaxes fresh fish up from the sea at the beginning of every good run. In southeast Alaska, to put it tactfully, lack of rain is not a problem. When I was growing up in western Washington I thought that fishing the Olympic Peninsula taught me everything there was to know about rain, but that was kid stuff. Parts of the Alaska panhandle get two hundred inches of drizzle every year. Now that's rain—*serious* rain.

But we are fly fishers here, not geographers or historians, so on to matters closer to the heart. It may help to review a list of things you can forget about on most southeast Alaska steelhead streams: elegant double hauls, encyclopedic collections of fly patterns, gentle runs flanked by user-friendly gravel bars. Here are things to substitute instead: industrial-strength rain gear, ankle-fit hip waders, tough tippets capable of turning over heavy flies in tight places and horsing big fish away from obstructions. No one ever said this was going to be pretty.

Which is probably why you don't hear more about Alaska steelhead fishing. Only a handful of Alaska streams are generally known in steelhead circles outside the state, but my own explorations have convinced me that virtually every drainage in the area supports at least some fish. Even the Alaska Department of Fish and Game admits that they haven't cataloged all the streams that host steelhead runs. Of course, it's probably better that way.

While some wildlife species thrive in proximity to man, to others we are distinctly bad neighbors. Wild steelhead fall into the second category. During the last ten years, steelhead returns have declined precipitously in the panhandle. Explanations for this phenomenon vary directly with the principal source of income of those doing the explaining, no surprise in a region in which logging and commercial fishing are two mainstays of the economy.

The Case of the Missing Steelhead is especially tragic because these are wild fish. Whether by shrewd intention, serendipity, or benign neglect, Alaska has by and large avoided the temptation of steelhead management based on the assumption that anglers will never know the difference. There is a hatchery on the Klawock but the area is otherwise free of fish factories, and the steelhead that return from the sea each year are unequivocally the real thing. When you bring a panhandle steelhead to bay in the shallows, you are looking at a product of the wild Pacific, not a hole in a punch card or somebody's PhD thesis. That should make each fish special when you find one, and it should make each one a cause for concern when you don't.

Back in steelhead country, I ease the truck to the side of the road and climb out into the cold, gray rain. A mile away at the bottom of the hill, a long finger of the sea insinuates its way inland to meet the stream, which, unlike Salmon Bay River, must remain nameless. When Ray and Doug and I first stood here a decade ago, the tide flat at the head of the bay might as well have been on another planet. We needed several attempts to find a way down through the maze of fallen logs and second-growth underbrush to the water, and when we had the route committed to memory, it was as if the little stream and the fish that it contained became our own private affair, a secret to guard jealously against the slow, steady press of the civilized world.

Few things are harder to hide than good fishing. Now a Forest Service trail runs from the road to the tideline, following our original route much of the way. Progress, I suppose, at least according to some definitions. At the trailhead, half a dozen empty bottles surround a charred log where someone tried to coax a warming fire from wood too wet to burn. A discarded condom lies on the ground like a viscid white comma. A cluster of beer cans sits crushed on the rocks. I begin to curse beneath my breath on general principle, but then I imagine what this drunken, rain-soaked coupling must have been like for its participants, and anger no longer seems appropriate despite the mess. At least they never made it to the stream.

I shoulder my day pack and move into the security of the woods, eager for the anonymity of the forest cover. The trail is so accommodating that it's hard to remember what this hike used to be like. Some of the brush here is literally impenetrable. Back then, no one visited the stream unless they really wanted to get there, which meant that almost no one did, except for a handful who knew of its hidden rewards. I never saw anyone there who had not come with me, and the occasional boot print in the sand felt more like a shared secret than violated trust.

Today, I am pleased to discover that the new trail winds on down toward the sea without crossing the stream itself. This means that I still have to thrash through a hundred yards of thick brush to reach fresh water, but the inconvenience is worth the privacy it provides. When I emerge at the first pool, the only tracks in the mud belong to otters and bears. Nature, it seems, is not yet ready to divulge her secrets to just anyone.

Even veteran anglers might have difficulty recognizing this stream as steelhead water. It moves, but it moves slowly, especially when the tide is high. It is so small that a novice could cast across it. Hell, most novices could probably *spit* across it. The first time I finally made it through the brush to this spot I was so disappointed that I nearly turned my back and walked away, but then I saw the long, sleek shapes finning in the current and the wakes left by new fish entering the tail of the pool on the incoming tide, and I discarded all my preconceptions and settled in for one of the wildest afternoons of fishing in my life.

Now the pool is quiet. The water seems opaque beneath the clouded sky, and I know I would be unable to see fish even if they were there, which is reassuring in a convoluted way. Today, the stream might be empty and it might be full, and there is no way to make the distinction except to go fishing.

The first pool fishes best from a little delta of sand where a feeder creek emerges from the brush. With some imagination, you can present a fly one way or another from that spot to just about all the good water in the pool without having to balance on logs or wrestle with the brush. I spend half an hour doing just that without turning a fish in the process.

Downstream, the going gets more interesting. There is plenty of holding water, but fallen logs crisscross the current like jackstraws, and getting a fly down to the fish requires careful attention to both the logs' geometry and the vectors of the current. There is nothing elegant about this stretch of water. To fish it, you have to think like a predator.

I work my way toward the tide for an hour, feeding a fly to the bottom of the stream every fifty yards or so. I see the otter that made the tracks upstream (or one just like it), and while no bears appear I can feel their presence; the pile of scat on one of the crossing logs is fresh enough to steam in the rain. Despite the apparent absence of fish, it's hard to call the trip downstream through the clutter a failure.

Finally I give up and hike back to the first hole, where the water is still quiet and too tempting to pass up. From the beachhead I cast upstream and dead-drift the fly down through the riffle at the head of the pool. Nothing. Then I cast across the current and let some classic wet-fly stuff happen against the opposite bank. More nothing. To end the day, I cast downstream and swing the fly seductively through the tail-out, where, on the third cast, the line hesitates and I strike and the tail of the pool comes to life at last.

What happens next scarcely matters. Plenty of others have written about screaming reels and leaping fish and I'm sure most of them can do it better than me. The important thing is simply that the fish was there, that it took the fly, that it revealed itself just when I needed a revelation.

As it happens I will land this fish, a bright hen of a dozen pounds or so with sea lice still dotting her belly. She will dance for me against the dark backdrop of water and brush before gliding to a stop on the sandy beach at the mouth of the feeder stream. There I will back the fly from the corner of her mouth, right her gently, and guide her back out into the current of her home water, the current she has sought for so long and with such determination.

When she is gone, I stand alone in the rain and marvel at the intricacy of convention by which I place myself in touch with what really matters. The hike, the fly, the fish—these are the things we do, and it's all just bloody marvelous.

For the pursuit of steelhead is above all else concerned with promises and their fulfillment. They promise to return and we promise to honor them when they do. The thesis is simple, its proof complex. And yet it is the exercise of that complexity that provides a final cadence to the relentless march of our lives.

Promises, promises. Who can dispute that if we kept ours as well as the fish keep theirs, the world would be a better place for all?

Chapter 2

Across the Inlet

 I found the king salmon hole by accident on a clear day in early July nearly fifteen years ago. I had spent the morning alone on a small Cook Inlet stream that used to afford some of the best fly fishing for kings I've ever experienced. I had fished most of the morning in solitude, taking two bright fish in the process. Neither weighed much over twenty pounds, small game by the standards of Cook Inlet kings, but they both turned aerial cartwheels and otherwise conducted themselves so well on the end of the line that no one could care how much they weighed.

By midday my casting arm was ready for a rest, and I hiked back upstream to the airplane. The air beneath the Cub's wings felt smooth and sensual as I departed for home. Free of obligations, I cruised leisurely down the wild side of the Inlet looking for things: moose, bears, fish, places to land an airplane. Eventually I passed across a broad glacial river and turned upstream toward its distant source in the Alaska range. Swollen with high water and glacial silt, the river itself was too inhospitable to fish, but hunting season was only weeks away, and I wanted to look over some gravel bars for potential landing sites.

Several miles inland a lazy little stream trickled across the muskeg and entered the swollen river. From the air the water looked clear as cold gin, and I could count the branches on the downed logs resting beneath the surface. A broad gravel bar shielded the stream's mouth from the river, forming a little estuary where the delicate water could rest before it surrendered to the rough surge of glacial current sweeping toward the sea. As I passed overhead, a pod of dark shapes tore through the clear water behind the gravel bar—*fish*, although I couldn't begin to tell what kind. My casting arm felt suddenly rejuvenated. Clearly, another look was in order.

I banked and made another pass with the low summer sun behind me. There was no doubt; the mouth of the stream was full of fish, perhaps an early run of red salmon heading upriver toward one of the many lakes in the drainage. In a country of turbid glacial rivers, no adventurous fly fisher can ignore the discovery of fish in clear water.

The gravel bar looked rough but manageable. The wind was blowing downstream, so I touched down right at the waterline and rattled to a stop at the edge of the willows. The great silence of the bush settled quickly, as I extinguished the familiar noises of the airplane one at a time and stepped out into the emptiness. The river grumbled past on its way to the sea but its dark waters held nothing to interest an angler, especially one carrying a fly rod, so I walked on down the gravel bar to the mouth of the little stream. In Alaska, fly selection is seldom an exact science. I tied on something bright and pitched it into the middle of the little estuary with the eager flush of excitement that comes from confronting mysteries in new water.

The streamer traveled less than a dozen feet before the rod tip yielded to a hard strike. The whole pool seemed to explode as my line circled its perimeter, then the fish headed for the river and the sea. I knew at once that if it reached the main current I would never land it. It did, I didn't, and there is nothing else to say about it.

I was fishing with stout tackle appropriate for big salmon, and this one had all but cleaned me out. Clearly, these weren't six-pound sockeyes. I replaced my broken leader and tied on another gaudy streamer. Three casts later a second fish struck. This one ran right past my legs on its way to the heavy current and its freedom. In the clear, shallow water, it was easy to identify the fish at last as a king.

I still needed to land one. Leader shyness is seldom an issue with anadromous fish, so I chopped off everything except a twenty-pound-test butt section, and served up another fly with true determination. When the line hesitated out in the current, I struck back as if I were fishing for tarpon. The salmon responded in kind, with a scorching run that tested my tackle to its limits. This time I applied pressure mercilessly and turned the fish just short of the glacial current. Fifteen minutes later I had the king on the gravel bar: a thirty-pounder, with just a blush of color in its flanks, still vigorous after the short run up from the sea, as imposing a specimen of gamefish as you'll ever see in fresh water.

I hooked another half-dozen kings before calling it a day. There were plenty of salmon left in the pool, but there comes a time when the point has been proven and it is best to get on with other business and let the fish get on with theirs. I felt enormously content as I walked back up the gravel bar to the airplane, but the wildness of the place wasn't quite through with me yet. Drawn by heat from the engine, mosquitoes covered the Cub's cowling like fungus. A thick fog of unwelcome insects swarmed inside the cockpit as I fired up the engine and waited for the prop wash to blow the bugs away. Perhaps the mosquitoes were simply nature's way of balancing the ledger.

Even so, how could I object? I know a good deal when I see one.

Captain James Cook was searching for the fabled Northwest Passage when he rounded the southern tip of the Kenai Peninsula on May 25, 1777. For the next several days, the log of the *Resolution* records a litany of fog, drizzle, squalls, and gales. The crew had never seen anything like the Inlet's tides; they could only run inland on the flood and hang on as best they could during the ebb. Even the eternally tolerant Cook became irritated over the loss of an anchor and hawser off what is still called Anchor Point.

An astute observer, Cook noted the debris flowing past on the outgoing tide and concluded that the Inlet terminated in a freshwater river rather than the Northwest Passage that he sought for the Crown. Others on board disagreed, so Cook sailed on against increasingly adverse conditions until the Inlet divided at what is now Anchorage. From there, he sent an exploratory party in each direction to confirm what he already knew. Leading the group that sailed up Turnagain Arm was none other than William Bligh, whose management shortcomings would eventually inspire the British navy's most famous mutiny and make Charles Laughton a movie star.

During the discouraged retreat from the Inlet, the Resolution ran aground on a hidden shoal near Kalgin Island, and only Cook's experience and seamanship saved the vessel from disaster. Although he did acknowledge the Inlet's "large quantity of very fine Salmon," Cook was plainly delighted to see the last of the place, as he admitted in his June 6 log entry:

> "I was induced, very much against my own opinion and judgment, to pursue the Course I did, as it was the opinion of some of the Officers that we should certainly find a passage to the North . . . Had we succeeded, a good deal of time would probably have been saved, but as we did not, nothing but a trifling point of Geography has been determined . . . ."

With that, Cook sailed on toward his own destiny on the beach at Kealakekua Bay, leaving it to his midshipman, George Vancouver, to return years later, complete the exploration of the Inlet, and name it in Cook's honor.

Today, two centuries later, the rugged coast that Cook explored is Alaska's most populated reach of salt water. Some things remain almost unchanged, however; the Inlet is still a vast source of unpredictable weather, raging tides, fine salmon, and surprises. It also serves as a line of demarcation between the roaded, settled, and (relatively) civilized Kenai Peninsula and our country's last remaining true wilderness, a mysterious expanse of glaciers, volcanoes, and tundra where few things ever turn out to be just what they seem.

Although stunningly beautiful by any standard, the land between the crest of the Alaska range and the Inlet's west shore is not easy country to enjoy, especially for the fly fisher. Access is difficult, the terrain rugged, and the brush merciless. Brown bears still outnumber people. Although fresh water abounds, much of it is all but unfishable, especially with fly tackle.

Fish taken there still come the old-fashioned way. You *earn* them.

It is late August, and the view from the air is breathtaking: the golden mosaic of dried grass on the tide flats beneath the airplane's wing, the defiantly snow covered peaks of the Alaska range sprawled across the horizon, the delicate arabesques of current traced upon the Inlet's icy waters. This is the season of caribou, sheep, and silver salmon. So much to do, but the days just don't feel long enough and I just don't feel young enough, not anymore.

The airplane is descending toward another glacial river, one that supports a fine but quirky run of silvers. This river passes through a series of broad, swampy lakes that act as settling basins. The lakes disperse enough silt and energy to make the lower river fishable even with a fly. Granted, dragging streamers through its turbid water is something of an acquired taste, but when the silvers are there in force they can compensate for a lot of aesthetic shortcomings.

And now the silvers are in. I proved that last night, keeping a bright dinner fish and releasing several more from an indifferent-looking stretch of water just above the tide flats. It is always tempting to return to the tried and true, but today I feel like exploring.

Even from treetop level, the water is too opaque to reveal any of its secrets. Several miles inland a nearly obliterated set of airplane tracks appears in the sand beside the river, and the run next to them seems as good a place as any to prospect for fresh fish.

As I circle to land, the airplane banks over an isolated backwater in the tundra. The water is slow and clear, and the unmistakable signature of porpoising fish marks its calm surface. Amazed, I come around again to confirm it, and then follow the waterway's meandering course through the grass. Expanding and contracting as it weaves its way along, it finally trickles into the main river nearly two miles downstream, establishing its integrity with the sea. The fish have to be silvers.

The original landing site is still the best I can do, so I flop the Cub down in the dirt and stand on the brakes until everything stops moving. There is the silence again, broken only by the easy rhythm of the river on its way to the sea. Armed with a fly rod and clad in hip waders, I secure the Cub in the willows and set off through the brush toward the great unknown.

There are places in Alaska that are fun to hike through, but the west side of Cook Inlet contains few of them. As soon as I leave the comfort of the sandbar I disappear into a hellhole of muck and brush. It is a hot day by Alaska standards, and my insect repellent is sweating off faster than I can apply it, a bit of intelligence not lost long to the mosquitoes. After half an hour of misery the question arises: Can fishing clear water really be important enough to justify this miserable hike? After another half hour, doubts about my own sense of direction surface, but there is the mountain peak I took my bearings from, right where it is supposed to be. Finally I stumble through a particularly unpleasant tangle of snags to discover my secret pleasure: a lazy black lagoon that looks as if it could be home to its very own creature, surrounded by line-tangling brush and teeming with legions of hostile insects.

The invitation is suspect, but after coming this far I am going to fish this pool if it kills me. Swatting bugs with one hand and wiping sweat from my eyes with the other, I finally manage to assemble my gear and find a place to stand that offers the possibility of a clear back cast. The pool remains quiet; perhaps the activity I saw from the air was just an illusion. Finally I work the line out overhead, fully prepared to take my lumps and begin the evacuation process at the first honorable opportunity.

The fly hits the water and disappears. The line eases gently toward the sea, establishing that there is some current here after all. My left hand strips slowly—once, twice, and then again. Suddenly the rod tip snaps toward the water with the unexpected force of a high-speed collision. Totally unprepared for this turn of events, I've got loops of loose line everywhere. One inevitably throws a half hitch around the rod butt, and when the fish runs it snaps the leader on impact and disappears into the cool dark recesses of the pool.

Stunned, I haul in what's left and look for clues, but find nothing but a cleanly broken leader. My internal focusing mechanism swings into action, and I see the water clearly for the first time since my arrival. There are dark shapes out there cruising just below the surface; I can see them now that I have come unburdened from my own sense of disbelief. I tie on another fly, gauge my back cast against the freshening breeze, and send the line across the water once more. There was something unusual about that first fish, something that will be defined only by catching one of its companions.

It takes a dozen casts this time, but then there is another savage strike. Thanks more to serendipity than to skill, the line runs free this time, and when the fish comes out of the water on the far side of the pool, the mystery is solved. The fish is a rainbow, a lean, bright bruiser intent on logging as much flight time as possible on the end of my fly line.

Even with stout salmon tackle, it takes some time to work the fish back through the clutter of snags that lines the pool. In hand at last, the fish confirms every expectation: five honest pounds, brilliant pink flanks, black markings crowded everywhere like medals on an old soldier's chest.

With the fish released at last, I feel like a prospector who just fell into the Lost Dutchman. You can always find nice silvers at this time of year if you look hard enough, but big rainbows are something special. In contrast to the legions of anadromous fish swimming upstream in cloned schools of hundreds, every rainbow has a character of its own to distinguish it from all others of its kind. And unlike salmon, they won't all be dead in a matter of weeks. When you release one, it is with the knowledge that you might actually get to see it again someday. You can make something personal out of fish like that.

The afternoon sun dips behind the peaks to the west as I hook a second fish and then a third and a fourth. Finally it is time to go. The long slog back toward the distant line of trees marking the river passes easily to the cadence of my bootsteps. A flight of teal guns by overhead as if they are enjoying the sound of the summer air rushing through their primaries. Water oozes slowly back into a set of brown bear tracks, but I pay them no attention. Even the mosquitoes seem tolerable. The fish have put me at ease with the country. Peace has been made once more.

A trip across the Inlet always feels greater than the sum of its geographic parts. Destinations there are defined by moods as much as by geography, and what you find there never loses its capacity to surprise. Thirty minutes of flight can transport you from the realm of the predictable into another era, where people must rely on themselves rather than things, on friends rather than institutions. The country there has all sorts of tricks up its sleeve, but it is never too proud to reward its visitors in unexpected ways.

Who knows what Captain James Cook thought as he battled his way back and forth against the Inlet's raging tides? Perhaps in the end he saw nothing there but another cruel joke at the hands of the sea, but I suspect he was enough of a dreamer to imagine what those treacherous currents might someday become: a body of water like the Delaware, the Jordan, or the Rubicon, whose crossing meant getting not just to another shore, but to another state of mind, where things are not so much what they seem as they are what you make of them.

Chapter 3

Saving the Best

Seals mean different things to different people. Biologists know them as efficient marine predators, commercial fishermen regard them as competition; to others, seals suggest the world of circuses and clowns. To me, on this particular day, the seal swimming in the lower reaches of southeast Alaska's Staney Creek meant that something out of the ordinary was about to happen.

It was early October, an edgy time of year in the north, with the feel of winter lurking just around the corner even on the most pleasant days. On two earlier visits to the stream that week we had seen eagles and gulls wheeling overhead as they fed on the rotting remains of the pink salmon run. A few dazed downstream humpies remained, turning listlessly in the backwaters, their backs picked raw by birds as they waited to join the carcasses of their predecessors piled in thigh-deep windrows by the tide. But we had come for silvers fresh from the sea, and we had yet to find them.

When my friend John Roseland and I pushed our way down the trail and emerged from the brush on the third morning, I saw the seal's head floating like a whiskered beach ball in the first pool above us. The seal saw us at the same time and tore wildly downstream toward the security of the open sea. No mammal swims with quite the authority of a seal in a hurry. This one looked like a gigantic parody of a gamefish as it torpedoed past us through the shallows, and the wake it left rocked the pool's shoreline long after its passage.

I knew there was only one reason for a seal to be this far upstream from salt water. As soon as the pool settled down, I climbed onto a broken log that jutted out over the stream like a diving board, and when I stared down into the tea-colored water through my polarized glasses there they were, dozens of dark green shapes as long as my arm aligned perfectly with the stream's even flow. When they turned, their sides flashed like polished metal in the sunlight, and I knew our search was over.

Now we had to catch some. To cast into the lie that held the salmon, we needed to be fishing from the gravel bar on the opposite side of the creek, so we hiked back down to the riffle where the seal had passed us. The incoming tide had pushed the water up against the banks, and we both went over our waders as we crossed, but we didn't care, not with fish like those waiting for us.

Once we established a beachhead on the gravel bar, I drained the water from my boots, shook like a bear, and began the painstaking process of selecting a fly: I reached into my belly bag and blindly retrieved the first pattern my fingers encountered in the fly book. It was big and bright and simple, and within minutes it was working its way along the even bottom out where I had seen the fish.

Spotting silvers in fresh water is both a blessing and a curse. Certainly it allows for more efficient fishing, but it also denies the excuse that the fish aren't taking because they aren't really there. The angle of the sun was no longer working in my favor and I couldn't see the fish themselves, but I knew they were still holding in the dark slick of water beneath the overhanging log, and that made the fly's first dozen uneventful drifts through the run difficult to understand.

There is a difference between a strike and a take, and when the rod tip finally went down hard there was no doubt that I had been *struck*. Then the fish was right there in front of me for an instant, clear out of the water, shining in the sunlight against the shadowed background of the undercut bank as if it were wired to its own power source. Then Rosey announced that he had a fish on, and the water churned with salmon in flight as the two hooked fish wrapped our lines around each other and then around a downed log for good measure. For a moment everything was complete chaos; then the pool fell still, except for a subtle flutter of activity beneath the surface as the fish settled back into place in the current and we reeled in what the two silvers had left us.

We took the loss of the fish in stride, because the sun was out (an unusual occurrence in southeast Alaska, and one that can compensate for all sorts of folly), because there were plenty of flies left and plenty of fish as well, and finally because there was just no reason not to. Then we regrouped and began to fish again.

We had been bowhunting blacktail deer all week, which meant hiking thousands of vertical feet into the alpine and eating out of cans at the ends of our long days in the mountains. We had yet to take a deer. Fed up with chili and peanut butter sandwiches, I wanted to cook something good and eat it and it was hard to imagine a more appealing candidate for the main course than fresh silver salmon.

Rosey hooked another silver and fought it relentlessly to the gravel bar. A twelve-pound male, the fish sported pink spawning colors and a generous kype even though we were barely upstream from the sea. Hailing from Montana, Rosey didn't appreciate the distinction between bright salmon and dark ones. He was about to dispatch the fish when I intervened. "It's been in the river too long," I explained. "It's too ugly to eat."

"We're talking about frying it," Rosey protested, "not taking it home to meet my mother."

I delivered a little homily about the virtues of bright fish on the table as well as on the end of a line that clearly left Rosey unimpressed. He did release the fish, however, leaving me to prove that we really could do better than past-prime salmon—or canned beef stew.

Fishing with intent to kill really does change the entire tenor of the experience, in ways both admirable and otherwise. While you certainly concede a measure of innocence, you also forfeit a unique intensity when the potential outcome of each cast is anything less than a fish on a plate. Arguing about catch-and-release with demagogues of either camp is about as productive as arguing about politics or religion, and I refuse to do it. Let's just say that anyone who slavishly follows any principle in the outdoors without regard to its biological justification is eventually going to miss out on something good.

So there I stood at the edge of the water feeling the sudden, unfamiliar *need* to catch a salmon, and the stream obliged me. It was another hard strike, and when the fish broke water I saw that it was just the one I wanted: mint-bright and just big enough to feed us without having to worry about dealing with leftovers.

Is anxiety about landing a fish good or bad for us? I'm not sure, but it certainly makes fighting one different. For a none-too-large silver, this one certainly upheld the honor of its species. There was lots of jumping and running around the pool while I worried about snags and knots, and Rosey reminded me how awful it would be if we had to eat crap again after he'd had a perfectly good salmon right in his hands.

Finally I eased the fish onto the gravel bar. The bedraggled remains of my streamer protruded from the corner of its mouth to emphasize the fragile nature of our relationship. So recently a proud, artistic product of the tying bench, the fly was now just worn-out hair and feathers, used once and spent as surely as a match or a mayfly. The sunlight played on the salmon's brilliant flanks, reflecting a perfect absence of color. The fish was almost too beautiful to kill. But not quite.

We spent another hour at the streamside catching silvers. With no reason to keep another I returned to the innocent mode of fishing, enjoying each strike and the show that followed for itself rather than as a prelude to some tangible result. It is not possible to say which provided more satisfaction, the one fish that I kept or the dozen that I released to continue their way upstream. But by the time we slogged back across the falling water to the trail some things seemed certain: The fish would all feed something before they were done, whether it was fishermen or seals or gulls; our art never endures the way we expect it to; winter will come and slam its door on all of us someday whether we want it to or not.

And finally, one last truth: sautéed salmon steaks taste better than canned chili.

Autumn is always my favorite season, especially in the far north, where its importance to the outdoors enthusiast is inevitably magnified by the grim authority of what is about to follow. Come September, the days are full of urgent reminders as diverse as velvet falling from caribou antlers in tattered bloody strips, the ponderous waddle of fish-fattened bears, and the gathering flocks of shorebirds along the beaches. They all know that nature is about to do something unforgivable to them, and after my first full year in that country I damn well knew it too.

Perhaps that's why the autumn equinox in Alaska always felt more significant than its vernal counterpart: At that latitude summer forgave indiscretions in a way that winter never forgave anything. And fall never lasted long enough, especially for someone accustomed to the drawn-out Indian summers of Montana's high plains. Factor in the staggering number of things to do at that time of year and the few short weeks you have to do them, and it's easy to see how the passage of summer can spell near hysteria among Alaskans, especially those determined to enjoy the outdoors. Of course there are things to do outside in Alaska during the winter, but none involves fly fishing.

To the fly fisher, nothing defines the relentless march of the seasons up north quite like the progress of the salmon runs. The kings come first, huge and brooding. Taking them on flies becomes a lot like hunting big game, with occasional epic flashes of excitement separated by long intervals of philosophy or tedium, depending on one's outlook on life. Next come the reds. Suffice it to say that fly fishing for red salmon requires its own personal commitment to a form of mental anarchy beyond the scope of this discussion. Then it's pinks and dogs, kid stuff and beginner's fare for the most part, and sometimes a downright nuisance when the streams are so choked with these species that it becomes impossible to fish for anything else.

Which brings us to silvers. Leave it to nature to save the best for last. *Oncorhynchus kisutch* demonstrates a number of characteristics sufficient to endear the species to the fly fisher's heart, not least of which is that silvers usually trickle into fresh water in dispersed and manageable numbers. While those unfamiliar with Pacific salmon may find the theoretical problem of too many fish difficult to imagine, the fact remains that we tend to prize what is somewhat difficult to find. Huge runs of salmon can overwhelm both sense and sensibility. That sometimes happens when pinks and reds are in the rivers and fish clog streams the way cholesterol clogs arteries. Schools of fish like that sound exciting, and they are the first time you experience them, but it's the kind of excitement that soon wears thin.

More to the point, silvers are the most inherently aggressive of the Pacific salmon species. They strike flies as if they mean business, and when hooked they can run and jump with the best of the competition. While they obviously lack the king salmon's bulk, they are larger than pinks and reds on average, and fresh silvers over fifteen pounds can test the limits of any fly tackle one is ever likely to use in fresh water.

All of which is not meant to suggest that silvers can't be moody enough to drive you crazy, because they most certainly can. Low water and falling tides often mean refusals even when the fish are there, but sometimes they just act coy for reasons known only to the salmon. Leader shyness is seldom the problem, and fly selection seems to have less to do with what happens out there than rational people probably want to acknowledge. Sometimes the best approach to a pool full of stubbornly uncooperative silvers is to go somewhere else and find fish that don't have headaches.

But you have to put *something* on the end of that leader, no matter how unscientific the selection process turns out to be. I've caught silvers on everything from single-egg patterns to Muddler Minnows, and virtually any steelhead fly or gaudy streamer will catch fish under the right conditions. My standard silver pattern remains a blue, green, and white streamer. Skeptic that I am, it took a long time at streamside to convince myself that the pattern was more effective than any other comparable bright attractor, but it is, and I have convinced most of my equally skeptical friends of this as well. Although it honestly didn't occur to me at the time I began fishing this fly, I believe that it imitates the little Dollies that are always gobbling eggs from the redds when migrating fish spawn, and that gamefish strike at it as a territorial reflex. At least this theory would explain the pattern's effectiveness on a wide variety of species that aren't supposed to be eating anything in the first place. Besides, every successful fly pattern deserves a theory of some kind, and this is the best I can come up with for this one.

Some people feel that smaller flies are more effective for silvers farther inland, and at certain times that is no doubt the case. The fact remains that anglers accustomed to the neatly constructed demands of matching the hatch on their favorite trout stream are going to have to adjust their thinking if they are going to fish for silver salmon without despair. Some years back my friend Ray Stalmaster illustrated the dilemma when he arrived from Montana for a week of September silver fishing.

"These fish come and go, don't they?" he began in a worried tone as we walked down toward the stream.

"Right," I replied.

"Then how do you know there are fish here right now?"

"Well, technically, I don't," I had to admit.

"And even if they *are* there, they aren't really eating anything."

"Right again," I said.

"Got it," Ray muttered, and then he spent half an hour flogging the water with grim resignation and looking like a man who would rather be doing something else, until he finally hooked a big silver that jumped all over the place and made a believer out of him.

And so my final bit of technical advice is to avoid worrying too much about the science (or lack thereof) involved in silver salmon fishing. In other words, just do it.

It is early October, and the river gliding by underneath the boat is the mighty Kenai. Moose season is over and most of the waterfowl are south of us now. An arctic high has settled in around us for the last several days, and along the banks the birches are dressed in gold as improbably rich in color as the azure sky overhead. This may be the last week of the ephemeral northern autumn, and we all want to squeeze as much from it as we can before it deserts us.

The Kenai seems worlds apart from the delicate little stream where our story opened. This is a big, brawling, broad-shouldered river, clouded with blue glacial silt and utterly indifferent to anything in its way. During the summer the Kenai becomes an inland marine highway, as tourists ply its swollen waters for the king salmon of their dreams and I go elsewhere to avoid the crowds. Now no one is left on its eerie blue water but a few diehards, romantics, and fools, and some of us probably fall into all three categories.

The Kenai will not give up its secrets as easily as Staney Creek, not by a long shot. There will be no telltale seals today, no overhanging logs from which to peer down and see the fish. So why am I pulling the boat up into this particular backwater? The answer is: *I don't know.* And you can take that to the bank.

The boat snubs up behind the anchor line and I begin to cast. If fishing for silvers anywhere requires optimism, fishing for them here requires a virtually religious level of faith. The river is so big, the fly so small. But I have been here before on days like this, and caught bruising silvers by the dozen doing just what I am doing right now. In the end it seems there is no basis for belief as reliable as experience distilled by human memory, so ready to retain the good stuff and filter out the rest.

The technical aspects of fly fishing glacial rivers are mercifully beyond the scope of this discussion. Suffice it to say that there are tricks to getting the fly down to where the fish are, or where we hope they are, and that it is seldom a delicate process. My heavy-tackle technique has been sharpened by another squandered summer, however, and today that part all goes easily. A hypnotic rhythm develops as I stand in the bow of the boat and cast, and even the first real nip of winter in the air cannot compromise my contentment.

Nothing much happens for a long time. On afternoons like this I sometimes find myself thinking more about *writing* about fishing than about fishing itself, and my instincts tell me this is a bad sign. Before this possibility disturbs me too much, the line hesitates out there in the current, defying the simple physics of the river's flow. By the time I set the hook and feel the fish throb on the end of the line I am very much back to thinking about fishing again.

Late Kenai silvers are often big fish. This one sure as hell is. Once it leaves the sanctuary of the backwater and reaches the main river's sweeping current, I realize that I have problems of the sort ordinarily reserved for king salmon season. I am using light saltwater tackle—an eight-weight rod with a #2 Fin-Nor reel—but the backing is melting down quickly. I could pull the anchor and follow the fish downstream, but that seems involved and touristy somehow, so I hold my ground right where I am.

One of the few friendly aspects of glacial rivers is the well-scrubbed quality of their bottoms. By the time a summer's worth of water has poured down the Kenai, there just isn't much left out there to foul a line. Sure enough, after a confused tour of the main channel my fish winds up in the backwater again, with line and leader none the worse for wear. We cavort around there for awhile until we're both about out of gas. Finally I slide the net under the fish and there it is, a bright and hefty hen with my fly gleaming from her lip like a misplaced emerald earring.

There will be half a dozen more fish this afternoon, but the numbers scarcely matter. It was the first fish that counted, the one that let me say a proper good-bye to the Kenai for the year. Somewhere out there winter is waiting to seal the river with ice, and now I feel that I'll be ready when the time comes.

It always falls to the silvers to remind me that there is no real difference between the end of one year and the beginning of the next. Perhaps that's why they return when they do, just when we need that reminder the most.

Chapter 4

Tideline

"Don't you miss the *mountains?*"

As a resident of the prairie I hear this a lot. The simple answer is *no*. In the first place I've got mountains, even if they're small, isolated ones rather than the sweeping alpine vistas of the coffee table magazines about the splendor of the Great American West. In the second place, the things that I really love to do in the mountains (elk and sheep hunting come quickly to mind) are largely activities that can be pursued in a manner more or less distinct from the rhythm of daily life. Finally, mountain terrain is often surprisingly barren, at least in comparison to the rich expanse of plains habitat that sprawls beneath the big sky around my Montana home. Mountains may be great places to visit, but I really wouldn't want to live there.

A lot of people are surprised by this answer, even when I take time to explain it. Most of them dismiss me as one of those vaguely addled characters who drives around eastern Montana in an old pickup with dogs in the back unable to imagine life without dust and sagebrush and shotgun shells, an opinion to which they are welcome.

But there's another geographic pole in my life, another ecosystem that I can inhabit without feeling compromised, and that is the coast of the Pacific Northwest. The cold tides of the North Pacific laid claim to my imagination when I was growing up in Seattle. Their influence reached all the way out here to the prairie awhile back, when I went to Alaska and forgot to return for six years. And I can still feel the tides' pull, even on a warm, still night when the coyotes are howling and the slap of the surf and the cry of the gulls are just memories.

Every year they call me back toward the sea, and in the good years I find ways to go.

Oncorhynchus keta is perhaps the least understood of the Pacific salmon species, at least from the sporting perspective. Little wonder. By the time they reach fresh water and fly-rod range, their flanks bear dark mantles of olive and maroon vertical stripes. With their exaggerated kypes and toothy grins, they look more like something you'd shoot in self-defense than catch for fun. Even their common names are unappealing: *chums* to shoppers and commercial fisheries interests, *dogs* to everyone else. That's why I settled into the habit of calling them *keta*, which is both their proper scientific and common Russian name. This fish can use all the help it can get from the marketing department.

Once you overcome the fact that dog salmon in fresh water look like dragon fry, *keta* have a charm of their own on the end of a fly line. They strike aggressively, run hard when hooked, and pack enough weight to test most freshwater fly tackle to its limits. In the process they take their place on an eclectic list of species, ranging from barracuda to northern pike, that happen to be worth catching on flies despite their fundamental ugliness.

It is late August, the season of mixed bags on the salmon streams of southeast Alaska. The water here on Prince of Wales Island runs sweet and clear, with none of the glacial silt that compromises the fly fisher's enjoyment of so many mainland Alaska streams. Giant conifers tower overhead, reaching up to tickle the belly of the thick, gray sky. A great nattering flock of gulls circles above the river, emphasizing our proximity to the sea.

Nick and Joe, ages twelve, lead the way through the eerie shadows of the old growth to the streamside. A tumult of bear tracks spreads across the sand, and piles of worried fish carcasses remind us that the bears came here for the same reason we did. The remains of the pink salmon run are everywhere—their bodies festooned across logs and rocks where high water deposited them earlier, the air ripe with the smell of decay. It's nature's way, I remind myself as my boots slide helplessly through a liquefying layer of pinks. For a moment, it is difficult to imagine ever eating salmon again.

Finally, Ray and the boys and I arrange ourselves at comfortable intervals along a gravel bar facing a dark, even slick of holding water. The surface is calm and there isn't enough sun to see fish, but you can sense their presence, just the way astronomers can sense the presence of an unseen tenth planet. It is time to test the hypothesis. One by one we finish rigging our rods and wade out into the current to discover what the sea has brought us.

At first it is largely a matter of ritual, the casting and mending of lines, the presentation of flies to fish that may not even be there. Ray and I are hoping for silvers. The boys don't really care what they catch, which is one reason why it's so much fun to watch them. They remind me of the time when I didn't know enough to be disappointed by anything on the end of a line either. I suppose my tastes have just grown more sophisticated, a change in attitude hard to characterize as progress.

A year has passed since I stopped giving Nick technical advice about his casting. Once they get to a certain point with the fly rod, kids become their own best teachers. Today he's working the line with authority. His form is still unpolished, but he has captured the elusive rhythm of the double haul, and his streamer sails easily across the deadwater into the heart of the run next to the opposite bank—childhood skills that will last a lifetime.

It seems that Nick deserves the first fish, and as soon as this occurs to me he has it. He shouts and the fish appears at the surface as if in response to his command—a looming calico figure with an undershot jaw, heavy enough to bend Nick's six-weight rod toward the water like a toy.

Nick badly wants to land this fish, so we all clear out of the water to give him room. On the end of a line, dog salmon tire quite easily despite their size, and once the first downstream run is over it's only a matter of time. Finally, Nick has the fish panting on its side in the shallows, and we all move in for a closer look.

"*Keta*," I murmur, cradling the fish gently. Nick asks for an explanation and I ramble on, telling him about the runs that choked the rivers in Siberia and how the Russians would strip the eggs from the gravid females, salt them lightly, and devour them on the spot. Joe moves his fingers across the fish's face, feeling the points of the teeth and marveling at their apparent ferocity. For a species no one seems to care about, this one offers plenty of wonderment to go around.

Nick releases the fish. I straighten up and retire to a log high enough above the waterline to be free of pink salmon carcasses. I don't need to catch *keta* today. I would rather watch the boys and wait for silvers on the next tide. We have been up since dawn, and my eyes slowly grow heavy. The last thing I remember is a dreamy chorus of seagull cries and the gentle sound of fly lines in the air. Then the morning sun breaks through the ground fog at last, and there is nothing to do but surrender to its warmth and close my eyes, imagining how I'll ever explain all this to someone who has never been here.

Here is a short list of things from the tideline that I miss when I am back in sagebrush country: salmon, steelhead, crab pots, sea ducks, butter clams, the sound of waves, blue mussels, driftwood, beach landings in the Super Cub, bottom fish, spring bears on the prowl, tide pools, starfish, the pervasive saline smell of the sea. It is worth noting how many of these things are good to eat, and of those how many go well with melted butter and cold beer.

A driftwood fire is crackling on the beach. Dinner is a huge bucket of steamers and, yes, there is plenty of all the ancillary supplies. The boys should be exhausted but they show no sign of fatigue. If the clams didn't taste so good, they would still be fishing. Rivers full of salmon can redefine the ordinary limits of fatigue, especially when you're twelve years old.

The water is calm and there are stars overhead—an uncommon state of affairs in southeast Alaska, where wind and rain are the norm and everyone gets a little giddy after two sunny days in a row. Here you learn to take advantage of weather like this, and so we are staying up later than anyone needs to, talking and working our way through the last of the clams and pitching the empty shells down the darkened beach for the next high tide to reclaim. It occurs to me that the social instincts of a subsistence culture have a direct relationship to the ease with which it can gather good food. No wonder the coast's native people were able to raise partying to the art form that became the potlatch.

Finally the clams are gone, the last one slurped down with a proper dollop of butter, garlic, and parsley from the bottom of the pot. A chill has settled around us as the earth surrenders its warmth to the clear sky overhead. My sleeping bag beckons. The kids are telling stories around the fire. I would like to stay up with them, but I am suddenly feeling both the years and the mileage.

I stand, gather up the clutter from our evening meal, and walk up the beach to the tent. Behind camp the forest looms, a dark, inscrutable presence. Entering the tent requires an awkward transition from outdoor wear to vulnerability, and for a moment I feel the way a snake must feel when it sheds its skin. Then the sleeping bag begins to glow with warmth, and I settle into its embrace for good as the rise and fall of the sea outside carries me off to sleep.

How can anyone get by without times like this? I wonder in the dark. And why would anyone want to?

Our five Pacific salmon species are as distinct as varietal wines, and I am always faintly amazed to find people who can't even tell them apart. Kings are huge and foreboding, their aura of mystery enhanced by the fact that they return first each year. Reds are brilliant, sporty, frustrating, and toothsome. Pinks and dogs are workaday fare on the end of a fly line, and smokehouse material when headed for the table. But if you want to see an experienced north country fly fisher look focused and intent, just offer a shot at the fifth species: the silver.

It is late morning, and a mile downriver the tide has started to fall. Here the stream is all deep lies and sluggish current, silver salmon water defined. There are no schools of pinks or dogs to intervene between fisherman and quarry. The water's surface is still and noncommittal. I like to think of silvers as the quiet salmon—quiet, that is, until you hook one on light tackle.

The tide has pushed the water up over the gravel bars, so I am perched precariously on a downed log like a bear. There is just enough room behind me to cast. I flip the streamer out across the sluggish reaches of the current toward the opposite bank and let it sink—down, down, and then down some more. The retrieve is barely enough to keep the fly moving across the bottom. Soon I am settled into the easy rhythm of salmon fishing, and the morning begins to pass by wonderfully overhead.

The essential quirk of casting to anadromous fish is that there may not be any of them there. You can't know unless you look, and the act of looking may in itself be an exercise in the absurd. To fish for salmon or steelhead effectively and without despair you have to accept this paradox and ignore its implications, like a character in a Beckett play. Then every take becomes its own reward.

And if you fish long enough and hard enough those rewards will come, as mine does suddenly after half an hour of addressing the impassive lie. The fly hesitates midway through its drift and my line hand hauls back, making contact. The subtle take is characteristic of a silver in deep holding water. Once the point of the hook drives home, however, you can forget all that quiet and subtle business as the rod bucks and the fish appears turning in the sunlight two feet above the water, chrome bright and fresh from the sea.

Two minutes later, it has taken me around a snag and parted from my company. No matter; this fish proves to be just the first of many. I can feel them moving into the pool now. The water level seems to rise to accommodate their volume, and there is a certain busyness beneath the surface that wasn't there before. Cold, wet fingers fumble. I tie on another fly, cast, hook a second fish, and cough this one right back up to the snag-choked stream as well.

For the next hour it is fly-rod salmon fishing at its best. I hook a number of fish and land a few. I intend to keep one small bright one for dinner, but somehow never quite get around to it. Then suddenly it's over. The salmon have moved on or changed moods according to their own agenda, leaving me with nothing to do but make a few final casts into the silent run, break down the rod, and call it a morning.

The fish have come and gone so suddenly, passing through my life with the odd clarity of a dream. It is amazing, really, that we should meet here together in the same place at the same time after all the thousands of miles we've traveled. It is amazing that I could cast to them with some odd concoction of feathers and hair and have them strike. It is amazing that the fish could give so much and ask so little in return.

Of course there is no place that amazes quite like Alaska.

Boredom is all but unheard of here at the tideline, where it seems impossible to run out of things to do.

The sea is calm, and we launch the inflatable boat easily through the timid surf. Ray holds us off with an oar while I drop the motor, which kicks sweetly to life on the first pull. I make a great science of picking a spot to fish, but it is all bullshit. We don't have charts or a depthfinder and there is nothing to do at the mouth of the bay but guess.

Fly fishing is such a consuming activity that it is easy to let it lead you astray. There are always fundamental issues to be worked out between fish and those who pursue them, and sometimes double hauls and the science of insect hatches can actually interfere with this process. Now we are back to basics: levelwind reels, 2/0 hooks, five-ounce leads, and hunks of herring. Suddenly everyone is a kid again.

I cut the motor in front of a rocky point and the baits disappear into the wine-dark sea. Less than a minute later both boys' rod tips are alive. The ocean is the final source of all mysteries, and none of us can resist the urge to lean out to see what's coming up from the depths. They are copper rockfish—spiny, ugly, and delicious. Stunned by the decompression of their rapid ascent, they lie comatose upon the surface until I scoop them over the gunwale and into the ice chest.

Thirty minutes later we have the makings of a world-class fish fry aboard, but the afternoon isn't quite over yet. There is one more favor I would like to ask of the sea before we head for shore.

Alaskans share a misunderstood disregard for salmon on the table. It's just that there is so damn *much* of it. I used to keep the first bright king of the year largely as a rite of spring, and an occasional fresh red if someone from "Outside" was visiting for dinner. That was it, except for subsistence fishing when I was out in the bush with nothing else to eat. All the rest went back, even though I love eating fish, and taking salmon in fresh water is of little biological consequence. I had just eaten too much salmon, thank you. There are limits to our tolerance even for the best of things.

If you want to honor an Alaskan with a fish dinner, serve halibut. Everyone loves halibut. Baked or fried, grilled or raw, plain or with any sauce that ever managed to complement a fish, its popularity is nearly universal. In contrast to salmon, halibut fillets and steaks are hoarded and doled out only on special occasions. Halibut can be bartered for almost anything. And the idea of fresh halibut in a hunting or fishing camp is almost overwhelmingly decadent.

And so I point the boat's bow back out toward the sea. The location of halibut holes is carefully guarded local knowledge, and as strangers to these waters we must rely on luck and guesswork. Five hundred yards beyond the last of the rocks, everything feels just right. The boys rig up and we begin to drift.

It is nearly slack tide, and the currents that customarily rage along the convoluted coastline are as still as they will ever be. The sun is shining, and the sea stretches away before us in a deceptive glassy calm. A sea otter's head appears off the bow, all whiskers and idle curiosity. It is easy to drift along with the last of the tide, enjoying the sun and trying not to think about what will happen if the outboard fails us.

Suddenly both rods are alive. No one is ready for this. Neglected drags squeal, lines circle the boat, all is chaos. The central question that always arises as soon as a halibut strikes remains: *How big is this thing?* After a few minutes of frenzy on the boys' part, it is apparent that both fish are in the manageable class, which is fine with me. Underequipped as we are, I'm not sure that we're ready for any two-hundred-pounders.

After five minutes of pumping, both fish hit the surface at once. Joe's promptly wraps his line around the motor shaft, which I have forgotten to raise in the confusion. That fish is history. In fact, one halibut is plenty, but that is a hard concept to get across to a twelve-year-old under such circumstances. No matter; our friendship will survive. We are without net or gaff, so I must grab Ray's shirt as he leans over and deftly tails Nick's fish. Joe's own disappointment fades before his fascination with our catch, the only vertebrate in the world that lacks a longitudinal axis of symmetry. We have done what we set out to do. The hunter-gatherers have hunted and gathered. With high fives all around we start the run back toward the shelter of the bay, where the frying pan is waiting.

The pace of life along the tideline is unique. The sea rolls out and the sea rolls in, and it always manages to bring something worthwhile right along with it. You can enjoy it with a fly rod or a clam bucket or a shotgun or a bow. Any way you cut it, this is kid country, and there is room for kids of all ages.

It is a long way from the prairie to the tideline. The wrack and swell of the sea are a distant memory here, where the fish have never seen salt water and the air is full of sage rather than the smell of the sea. But I can still feel the tides pulling. Honest.

Mountains? Forget them. You know where the prairie's rival for my heart lies now, just as surely as you know why.

Chapter 5

Lifeblood

 Rivers, like people and good stories, come in order, with beginnings, middles, and ends. Human lives are laid out along the continuum of time, but flowing water enjoys another organizational option: space. (We shall ignore for now the anti-Newtonian notion that there is no difference between the two, although rivers sometimes remind me of this principle with as much clarity as any natural phenomenon I know.)

The defining feature of rivers is motion, from which everything wonderful about them derives, including the fish we love to catch and the habitat necessary to sustain them. Rivers are the indentured servants of gravity, and as that mysterious force sweeps them along they pass through predictable stages of maturation, from the babbling childhood of their headwaters to the inevitable senescence of their merger with whatever larger water is destined to consume them in the end. And no two parts of the river will ever be the same, even though they are scarcely parts at all but aspects of an almost vital entity joined together as seamlessly as the sides of a Shaker box.

Fly fishers should appreciate these matters, although we often fail to, probably because we use the wrong conjunctions when we think about rivers and our approach to them. If you say that you are going *to* the Kenai to fish for silvers, that implies that your destination is a point in the geometric sense, which cannot be the case. We need to school ourselves to go *upon* or *along* instead. That would be a start.

The definitive way to retool your thinking about these matters is to float the rivers that you love, and to think of floating every time you think of the water, even if you do so subliminally. Float trips have beginnings and ends just like rivers themselves. While afloat, the angler is subject to the same forces as the water, which establishes an intimacy denied those on shore. Floating allows the fly fisher to feel what the fish and the mayflies and our imitations feel. It is a form of surrender that lets us become part of what we seek.

Relatively few rivers, however, allow even the ambitious explorer the opportunity to experience them from beginning to end, from birth to death if you will, at least if fly rods are a significant part of that exploration. Rivers large enough to float (and I suppose that floatability is as practical a definition as any of a river, as opposed to a creek or a stream) generally require some time and distance to get from one end to the other, which means that floating their length requires commitment and planning. Most rivers are too small near their origins, or too boring in their lower regions, or something. And in the developed part of our country, which regrettably is to say almost all of it, it is hard to find a river that hasn't been hopelessly defiled somewhere along its course.

The ideal is a wild river that will let you travel right along with it from its origins until it finally lies down to sleep. Travel with a river like this and you will be a different person at the end of the journey than you were at the beginning. And nowhere are there rivers that let you experience this transformation of the spirit quite like Alaska.

There is no silence so impressive as the silence that lingers after the departure of a float plane in the bush. Now the Beaver's great radial engine roars and recedes slowly beyond the horizon, and then there is nothing but the sound of the wind. Suddenly and utterly alone, we look at one another: Ray, the two boys, and myself. We are our own resources. The food we brought is what we will eat for the next ten days, except for what we catch or kill or gather for ourselves. We will have to get along no matter what. We always have, but the rules of engagement are different now. Out here, the most trivial offense can escalate into unimaginable bitterness. It is our responsibility to ensure that this never happens, and as we study one another we promise silently that it never will.

And then the work begins. The skies are clear, the tundra underfoot dry and inviting, but we have no time to enjoy any of this now. There is gear to be carried from the lake to the banks of the tiny outlet stream. The rafts need to be inflated, the dry bags packed and packed again. Of course there's really no hurry, but we are still fresh from the world of schedules and deadlines. Give us a day or two. That's all it usually takes.

Finally Nick and Joe straighten from the pumps, and it is time to launch the rafts at last. The commitment of a vessel is customarily a ceremonious occasion, calling for a bottle of champagne, oohs and aahs from the assembled throng, and a stately settling of the craft upon the water until Archimides' principle is satisfied. This afternoon there are problems. We have no champagne, the participants are all too busy swatting bugs to ooh and aah at anything, and the rafts are nearly as wide as the stream, which means that true flotation is impossible. Eighty miles of this? Ray wonders aloud. Goddamn right, I bluster back. Nick and Joe, now fifteen, are still young enough to believe that their fathers can see them through anything, a flattering sense of optimism that I truly wish I could share.

Finally there's nothing left to do but load the rest of our gear into the cargo nets slung fore and aft across the rafts and shove off, even though it is impossible to suppress the notion that getting into the tiny stream is a lot like getting into a bathtub. Here at the headwaters we are traveling across open tundra, so there are no blowdowns to battle our way through and I know we should be thankful for that. Still, the first mile passes slowly as we walk the rafts downstream through the shallows.

Our principal goal on this trip is actually not fly fishing but the pursuit of caribou with the bow. Of course, saying that we are not really interested in the fish is sort of like saying that you aren't really interested in your girlfriend's body: It sounds honorable, but nobody could possibly believe it. And there are fish in the outlet stream, even though it scarcely seems big enough to contain them. We can see them scrambling for cover in the gin-clear water as we clatter by awkwardly overhead. They are grayling, small fry for the most part and certainly too small to cause any real excitement. Besides, as organizer of this expedition I am full of misplaced urgency to get on down the line, to feel some real current rise beneath us, to go to bed knowing that we won't really have to drag the rafts through eighty miles of low water after all.

The river is gathering itself right out of the high tundra all around us. Freshets join us at every bend, like kids tagging alongside a parade. At last there is enough water to float the rafts, and then to float the rafts with us sitting on them. Finally we arrive at a confluence with another lake's outlet stream and the water broadens about us; we feel like we are on a real float trip at last.

A small band of caribou crosses the rolling hills ahead, but Alaska's same-day-airborne hunting restrictions mean we can only watch. The last of the wind dies and the bugs arrive in determined clouds, aggravating us not so much by biting as by flying like kamikazes into our ears, noses, and eyes. I come with a high tolerance for bugs, but these are trying my patience, especially the ones that seem determined to crawl beneath my contact lenses. It's their tundra, I remind myself philosophically. I am the one who must come to terms with them.

Ray and Joe are a hundred yards ahead of us when the ravens rise from the willows along the bank. Ravens do not gather in open country without a reason. The reason is often something dead, and in grizzly country carrion seldom goes undetected by grizzlies. No sooner have I explained this important exercise in logic to Nick than the bears show up on the open hillside just above the river, spooked from the cover by human scent from the lead raft. It is a sow and two yearlings, and as they lope easily up and over the nearest hill I am reminded how beautiful bears in motion can be, especially when their motion is carrying them away from the observer.

Our goal for the first night is simply a campsite on dry ground with enough exposure to let the wind carry the bugs away, and as the long northern twilight fades overhead, we find it. The river is calling, but by the time we have made camp we are all just too tired and hungry. Dinner comes slowly to life on the Coleman stove, its warm, drippy smell wafting out across the tundra, a two-mile-long invitation to the bears. I know I will sleep lightly tonight. Tomorrow belongs to the river.

Although it has grown large enough to accommodate the rafts, the river is still little more than a trout stream, clear and inviting but somehow too small for the sprawling country around us and the outsized fish we hope it contains. Something seems to be missing, however. Turn this inviting current loose on the high plains of Montana and the air above it would teem with welcome bugs: mayflies, caddis, stones. You know, trout food.

Here the nurturing of fish ultimately depends upon the distant bounty of the sea. The ecological bottom line is that our river cannot make it on its own; the growing season is too short, the flow of biochemical energy too constricted. The hard part of the algebra—getting the goods from the sun and into the food chain—ultimately takes place in the distant, fertile waters of Bristol Bay, where it would all remain but for the salmon. They have been arriving in specific waves all summer: kings, reds, and dogs, reduced by now to downstream wanderers and carcasses rotting in the sun. It is hard to appreciate them now that they stink and crawl with worms, and even the less discriminating scavengers seem to have lost interest in their remains. But remember: Without them none of us would be here, for the river would be barren.

And now, for those readers grown edgy because we are midway through our story without so much as a token appearance by a real gamefish, they appear as soon as there is enough sun on the water to let us see into the corners of the deeper pools. At first they are mere suggestions of themselves, tantalizing gray shapes that may or may not be fish, pricking the imagination before they disappear into the shadows on the bottom of the stream. Finally their presence is undeniable, and we pull over to the bank at the head of a long, inviting run and break out the fly rods.

The fish are grayling. As soon as I cast, one detaches itself from its holding lie along the bottom and attacks my fly, an Egg-Sucking Leech. While my sentimental regard for grayling is a matter of record, I ordinarily don't get too excited about their performance on the end of a line. However, this is a solid specimen of two and a half pounds or thereabouts, and since I have had the foresight to pack my five-weight rod rather than my usual brawny salmon outfit, the fish out there in the current is more than enough to keep me occupied.

No matter how many times I've been through this, I just can't land the first grayling of a trip without stopping to take a look. Beached at last, my fish suggests some futuristic sculpture as it lies on the wet gravel with its improbable dorsal fin on display. Eerie violaceous hues appear and disappear in the sunlight as if by magic. I study the fish intently in an attempt to define them but I cannot, and then I reach for the camera in the day pack, although I know those colors will elude the film as well. There is a time to struggle in the pursuit of natural mysteries and there is a time to accept them. Recognizing the latter when I see it, I unhook the fish and slide it back into the current and that is all.

Downstream, the boys are calling excitedly. Both have hooked grayling, the first of many from this pool, itself the first of many during this long arctic day. I straighten slowly from the gravel and walk downstream to join them, wondering about the fish I have released and whether any medium can ever contain that blush of purple on its sides.

It is late in the afternoon. We have made camp where the river cuts through a wasp-waist in the hills. From here we can climb in either direction to the high country in search of caribou. Six dozen grayling into the day, I really don't need to fish anymore, but something about the run in front of camp makes it impossible to walk away. Beside me on the gravel bar Ray is studying the water intently, and I can tell that he feels it too. Finally we leave the boys to sharpen some broadheads before the evening hunt, while we retrieve our gear from the rafts and wade out into the river.

The grayling are there as expected. I have hooked and landed another unnecessary half dozen when an anomalous shape appears briefly in the current, but the low afternoon light refuses to define it further. I remove and replace my polarized glasses and walk up and down the bank trying to solve the essential trigonometry between the sun, the river, and my retina, all to no avail. Finally the shape appears again: a dark, undulating absence of gravel on the river's gravel bottom appended by a delicate white marking that I am willing to accept as the pectoral fin of a char.

I dig a single-egg pattern from my fly book, lead the shape's last known location by a dozen feet upstream, and cast. Several drifts later the line hesitates, and I set the hook into something that is clearly not another grayling. For five minutes the fish remains an official mystery at the bottom of the run, fighting with less flair than determination. Meanwhile, fifty yards upstream, Ray is fast to something similar. Finally, I get my fish up in the shallows: It's a five-pound Dolly. I release the fish and slog upstream toward Ray. His fish turns out to be another Dolly, a larger specimen that looks as if it could push eight pounds if anyone cared enough to weigh it. Vividly dressed in its fall spawning colors, it may be the most beautiful freshwater fish I have ever seen.

Enough is enough. Back in the camp the boys are getting fidgety. Ray and I walk up the bank, peel out of our waders, and exchange fly rods for longbows. Ray volunteers to hunt across the river while I accompany Nick and Joe up the mountain in back of camp.

Two hours later, Nick and I are perched high in the tundra with our binoculars pressed against our faces. We have seen a handful of caribou, none of them mature bulls, and one brown bear. I swing my glasses back down the hill toward camp and there is Ray, a solitary figure in the middle of the stream, the last of the sunlight sparkling on his fly line as he casts. He hooks a fish immediately, and I watch as he plays, lands, and releases it. Then he hooks another one. And another.

Evidently, enough is not enough after all.

After consulting the topo maps the following morning, we are ready for the river to flex its muscles and carry us on down the line. We are no longer dragging bottom, but we aren't moving very fast either, and we have a long, long way to go. Every mile or so we pick up some little tributary from the hills. As each stream joins us, we can feel the water swelling underneath the rafts, lending its momentum to our progress. Then the river starts to break up into shallow channels as it spills out of the high country and spreads across the open tundra, and by early afternoon we are walking the rafts downstream again. Now we can consider the implications of being delayed for days, missing our pickup and running out of food, or we can go fishing. Out come the fly rods.

This river isn't as famous for rainbows as some of its neighbors, but that's just because it's hard to get to, which obviously is just fine with us. We know there are rainbows here somewhere, tucked in between the grayling and the silver salmon waiting downstream. We also know that if we keep fishing for them long enough, we're going to find them. After two days on the river I am ready for the rainbows, which need neither the grayling's dorsal fin nor the Dollies' vivid colors to establish their credentials on the end of a fly line.

I am taking pictures of Nick fishing the head of the pool below our third night's camp when the first rainbow appears. He has been catching grayling on every second or third cast when something smashes the streamer out in the cool dark current and heads downstream with more determination than any grayling. We both recognize the fish as something out of the ordinary even before it jumps and flashes its pink flanks in the arctic evening's eerie light. Getting the four-pound fish to shore is a long proposition on light tackle, but Nick finally brings it up short in the shallows for us to admire. Radiating energy like a live coal, the fish looks just the way a trout should look here in this lonely world of survivors.

One thing is for sure: The fish is still a survivor when we're done with it. Released from the streamer's bite, it flicks its tail and disappears into the river, leaving us both faintly amazed at the ability of one small cold-blooded creature to change our entire perception of the evening. Once the fish is gone, I store the camera away in my day pack and retrieve my own fly rod from its resting place in the willows. I want a rainbow. Nick wants another rainbow. It is time to ask the river for a favor, and as it turns out neither of us will be disappointed.

The water swells all around us, maturing like a teenager with each passing mile. The grayling lag behind and disappear, and then the char are gone as well. The river's south fork joins us, doubling the pulse of water beneath the rafts as we spill out of the hills and onto a broad tundra plain. We are making real progress now, so much that I wonder aloud why we ever imagined we were in a hurry.

For several days we are distracted by bows and arrows and caribou. Then I've got a bull down; we can stop worrying about having enough food and I can fish again in peace. We are approaching the river's lower reaches, and it is time to start thinking seriously about fresh silvers.

The river serves up its salmon in tantalizing little hints of what might lie in store. The remains of the king salmon run appear first, great rotten hulks lying randomly about the banks like victims of a terrorist attack, so foul by now that even the bears won't bother with them. Then comes what's left of the *keta*, wandering downstream after spawning. They are literally more dead than alive, betrayed by some genetic time bomb programmed to self-destruct as soon as they finish the business of reproduction. The fish seem indifferent to their fate. I am moved by the promise of their death, but there is nothing to be done, so we pass each other in silence.

We drift right on through miles of this bio-pageant, glassing for game and picking up an occasional rainbow. What I want, though, is a fresh silver, which is why I am balanced precariously in the bow of the raft peering into the depths of each new pool as we pass overhead. It is a sunny day, but the angle of the light is tricky. Images coalesce and disperse against the mosaic pattern of the river bottom, always disappearing just before I can confirm them. Then we drift around one more bend and into a broad pool choked with fish.

They are silvers of all persuasions, from crimson-sided, hook-jawed monsters to sleek, bright fish that look born to perform on the end of a fly line. Caribou and rainbows forgotten, we pull the rafts out on the nearest gravel bar and rig for salmon. In minutes all four of us are sight-casting toward the teeming schools, each braced against the inevitable first strike and wild run.

But there are points to be made on nature's side of the ledger today, the first being that nothing involving fish and fly rods is inevitable. The silvers won't hit. Why? Hell, I don't know. As an experienced Alaska angler, I suppose I should be able to come up with some explanation, but I can't. And so the great mass of fish circulates about the pool in front of us with absolute indifference while we change every variable at our disposal: big flies, small flies, dark flies, bright flies, fast retrieves, slow retrieves, dead drifts—the fish ignore them all with maddening insouciance. Then Ray inadvertently hooks a dark specimen in the tail. By the time he thrashes the fish into shore and releases it, we all realize at once that we have no more business with these salmon.

After days of technically easy fishing, perhaps we needed this reminder: The essence of the sport is not the catching but the pursuit, a distinction that can be defined only by occasional failures. On balance the river has certainly been more than fair to us, which is why we are all still in good spirits as we ease the rafts back into the current. Below us, the silvers glide by unconcerned. Whatever our problem may be, it isn't theirs and they seem to know it. There are hundreds of fish in the pool, averaging ten or so pounds apiece. Simple math confirms that we have been casting to gamefish by the ton.

But today we might as well be inhabiting a separate world, as if the river's surface is a boundary we cannot cross. The salmon move upstream and we move down, and then I lose the light and the fish are gone. In its own way, our failed connection is as tangible as all the contact between angler and fish that happened earlier. I will remember it just as long and consider it just as deeply, and in the end that may be all that really counts.

Two days later we round another bend and join the Bristol Bay tributary into which our river flows. The water is all different now: duller, warmer, slower, bigger. There are still fish out there in the current, but I'm indifferent to their possibilities. I have lost my heart to the river we just left.

It was seeing the river through from beginning to end that did it. How remarkable to note the number of ways by which we could measure our progress: miles, days, moods, flies, fish. The fish were as certain as any in the end, marking each phase of the journey from eager grayling in the high country to fickle silvers out on the tundra plain. Win, lose, or draw, all the parties treated one another fairly and each of us can be proud of that.

There is no better way to learn a river than to do what we have done, and what we have learned is that rivers like this are lifeblood to us all—fish, fishermen, the country itself. The rest will go better now. I just know it.

P a r t I I

MONTANA

When I was in the fifth grade I fell in love not once but twice. The first object of these confused yearnings was a girl named Patty Sherman. The second was Montana.

I don't know what happened to Patty. I can't remember what she looked like and I couldn't pick her out of a lineup, but in the unlikely event that she became an avid enthusiast of outdoor literature and happens to read this, she's sure welcome to give me a call.

I did better with Montana, although it took another twenty years to consummate our affair.

We lived back in northern New York in those days, but my father was smart enough to appreciate the value of loading the family into the station wagon, strapping the canoe on top, and heading west, where the sky swept high overhead and the streams held more than six-inch brook trout. We had been to Yellowstone and Glacier before, but it was the trip we took the summer after I finished fifth grade that finally made me recognize the pole toward which my internal compass would point for years to come.

The thing I remember most about that trip is the intense anticipation engendered every step of the way. I saved my trapline money that year and ordered a new fly rod, a fiberglass Shakespeare Wonderod that at the time seemed the most marvelously decadent tool a fish-happy kid could possess. The order went out well before our scheduled departure, but the rod didn't arrive; my last week in town consisted of one disappointing daily trip to the mailbox after another. The day we were scheduled to leave I talked my father into waiting for the morning mail, and there it was. Opening the package felt like taking communion.

Then there was the interminable drive across the Midwest. My brother and I read and slept to the welcome rhythm of the highway while my parents drove in shifts around the clock. Every morning we awoke to a new monotony of farmland gliding past the windows and alien license plates beside us on the road: Ohio, Iowa, South Dakota. It may sound like a convincing argument for air travel, but in retrospect I wouldn't have missed it for the world.

Finally, jackrabbits and sagebrush appeared beside the road like flotsam alerting sailors to an impending landfall. We began to study the western horizon in earnest, and when we woke up the next morning blue mountains lay stenciled there among the clouds. The license plates on the passing cars said *Montana*, and we knew we had arrived at last.

The odd thing is, I can't remember much that happened afterward. There was lots of fishing and no Patty Sherman, and if I had correlated these two facts with my general sense of rapture perhaps I might have saved myself all sorts of heartaches in the end. As things went, I simply decided that Montana was the place for me, which represented pretty clear thinking for a kid that age with lots of trout on his mind.

I always knew that I would come back to stay and I did. Fish weren't the only reason, of course (let's see, there's grouse and elk and antelope . . .). Still, it's hard to distinguish the idea of living in Montana from the idea of fishing in Montana, an association that has cost me a couple of marriages and an incalculable amount of money over the last twenty years, and which I would not reconsider even now, knowing everything I know. It's the people that disappoint you in the end, not the fish.

With all the good trout habitat scattered around, it's hard to articulate what makes Montana so special to those of us who care about these things. It can't just be the fish or the scenery, because you can find both in other places that evoke far less emotion than Montana. The same goes for the weather and the bars and the beef, all of which are enjoyable but not qualitatively different from their counterparts elsewhere. It's not solitude, as anyone knows who has fished the Madison or the Big Hole lately, and you can forget about all that unspoiled western splendor, at least if you're flogging the water on a tailwater fishery like the Big Horn or the Missouri. (Spoiling western splendor happened to make those places work as trout water, which is one reason I don't like them. But that's another story.)

To me, the defining features of the Montana fishing experience are the water and the sky.

Trout streams here know how to pace themselves. Their gaits seem appropriate to the circumstances, brisk enough to keep the action going without really hurrying. The water runs clear but not too clear, an important consideration for those of us who don't necessarily enjoy staring our trout in the face and who like our streams to hold secrets as well as fish.

Despite these common characteristics, the variety of water available here is staggering. A few hours' drive from Bozeman or Ennis or Twin Bridges encompasses enough good trout water to keep an ambitious angler occupied all season, with a menu that varies from delicate spring creeks to brawling rivers. Let's face it: Sometimes you feel like technical dry-fly fishing and sometimes you feel like pitching junk. No matter what your mood or ambition, Montana has water to accommodate you.

Paeans to the Big Sky are hardly original; hell, there's one on my license plate. Nonetheless, it's hard to appreciate just what that sky means until you spend some time under it and then some more time away from it. When I left Montana, it was the sky I missed the most, just the way I missed Alaska's light. It manages to be both beautiful and imposing, reminding us simultaneously of our limitations and possibilities. And there it is right outside my window, waiting to remind me of both the next time I go fishing.

So that's how I frame the Montana fishing experience: water and sky, two of the four primal elements forged into a unique setting for the rituals between fish and fishermen. It's a romantic notion, and one that may be hard to keep in mind when the browns are making fools of you on your favorite spring creek or the crowds are surging by during the Outfitter Hatch on one of the Blue Ribbon streams. But then Montana is a romantic place. I've known that ever since the fifth grade.

And I'll stand by my guns.

Chapter 6

Caddis by Night

We put in at Dick's house late that afternoon with the idea of drifting right on through the middle of town. Since the town in question was Livingston, Montana, this plan had more merit than most proposals to float through the middle of a town, but the noise and the busyness all around us still felt unsettling. The summer had been wet and the river was high even though August was just around the corner. Junk—the usual staple of midday fishing on the Yellowstone at this time of year—had not worked earlier, and there was no reason to think it would now. Muddlers and Woolly Buggers and allied exercises in bad taste produce reliably on the 'Stone when you can get them to the fish, but the edges of the river were still up in the willows, and casting there from the driftboat somehow felt like a waste of time and proved to be just that. But we couldn't forget the events of the previous evening, when the caddis appeared on the water at last, the trout rose from the unruly depths to consume them with abandon, and we caught browns and rainbows until the light faded from the western sky and broke our hearts as it disappeared.

High water changes all the rules of the game. It should have been easy to walk down to the boat and get in with no gymnastics, but the surge of current shooting downstream from the Park made that impossible. Dick steadied the boat from shore while I climbed over the side and sat down at the oars, and then Annie held the boat while Dick lunged into the bow. When she pushed us off and waved good-bye, the current swept us away and we felt the responsibilities of life recede behind us.

Dick fished his standard Yellowstone River cocktail—a Royal Trude preceded by a large Hare's Ear on a dropper—for half a mile without a hit. Finally I pulled over on a flooded gravel bar and we both got out to work the riffle next to it. I pitched a George's Brown Stone nymph into the broken water for twenty minutes without so much as a suspect bump from a whitefish, then we started downstream again. The river really left us nothing to do but cast halfheartedly against the bank and wait for darkness and the great perhaps.

As the shadows began to stretch across the water and lose their definition, I braced myself against the boat, clipped off whatever nonsense I had been fishing, and tied on a deer-hair caddis pattern. No fish were rising yet, and my choice was based more on logic than data. By this time it was either going to happen with caddis up top or it wasn't going to happen, period.

Livingston's tender underbelly was sliding past us on the lefthand bank when the first fish finally struck. The fly was hard to see despite its buoyancy and the generous outline of its wing, but suddenly it was absent longer than current and light could account for and I struck. The fish was an acrobatic sixteen-inch rainbow, and it did everything it was supposed to do. "You're up," I told Dick when I finally leaned over the side and released the fish.

We traded places as the current pulled the boat around in an eddy, and by the time I straightened up behind the oars it was clear that something strange and terrible was happening all around us. The river was suddenly alive with feeding fish, the same river that had greeted our earlier efforts with such impassive silence. Dick had an immediate strike on the dry-fly half of his tandem rig, and he fought the fish to a draw while I ran us aground on another flooded gravel bar. Then we were both out in the current on foot, surrounded by the steady surge of high water and more eager trout than either of us could have imagined.

Under ordinary circumstances the riffle would have been an awkward affair to fish, since the water broke unevenly over the bar and swept around in circles without ever offering the sort of smooth, laminar flow that seems to beg for a fly line. That night, it simply didn't matter. It didn't matter where you stood or where you cast or, within the broad limits of accuracy defined by caddis patterns, what the fly looked like upon arrival. It didn't matter because the Yellowstone's rainbows had all gone crazy at once. I caught a second fish and remembered teen-aged girls fainting at Beatles concerts in the sixties. I caught a third fish and imagined medieval French peasants gone mad from hallu-cinogenic rye. I caught a fourth fish and dreamed of mindless riots at soccer games. By the time I landed the fifth fish I had exhausted my supply of analogies to describe collective hysteria, and there was nothing to do but keep on fishing mindlessly. Anyone capable of tying a #14 dry caddis pattern to the end of a leader and hitting the water with it could have caught a lot of nice trout; that Dick and I each did so isn't exactly an accomplishment that belongs on our resumés. This bothers some people who really ought to know better, as if fish don't really count unless catching them involves consternation. The joyful ease of it all sure as hell didn't bother me, not after all those long, fishless miles on the river. I felt like a hog in a pile of ripe garbage. The way I saw things, we had paid the price of admission.

That we were fishing the Yellowstone certainly helped erase any guilt that might accrue from the staggering number of fish we were catching. The 'Stone is a tough river that makes its enthusiasts suffer as much as any body of water I know. It is also home to more *big* fish per mile than any other river in Montana, and every cast was tempered by the under-standing that something truly huge and unforgettable might come up out of the gloom and smack my little deer-hair caddis at any moment. This is just the kind of possibility that motivates guys like me to fish rivers like the Yellowstone, and to keep on fishing them even after they have spurned my advances for days on end.

The browns never even made an appearance. I don't know why the mysterious cues that trigger fish to feed are so species-specific, but we didn't raise a single brown that night, or a single cutthroat either, as if whoever issued the invitations to the party meant to snub them. It would have been nice to see some dull amber flashes out there in the darkness, but with all those rainbows, complaining about the lack of brown trout seems positively selfish.

The sun's dull glow was fading from the western sky, and the lights of town rose slowly to challenge the darkness left behind by its depar-ture. Artificial lights ordinarily bother the hell out of me outdoors, and have even inspired an occasional act of vandalism, but on this particular evening they were little more than a distraction. They made me feel invisible somehow as I fished on, content in the knowledge that I could see the town but the town couldn't see me, while I stood right in the middle of Livingston and caught fish that the people on the other side of the lights could scarcely imagine.

The noise of feeding trout rose above the sound of the current out in the darkness, and when I cast next, I closed my eyes and listened for the particular sound of one fish rising to my fly above the rest of the hullabaloo, like the sound of one hand clapping. Then that sound was there and I struck, and the rod jumped in my hands as if to confirm that I had established some private language with the river. This was getting spooky.

And when it comes to fishing that is spooky, as opposed to simply good or fast or memorable, I note with surprise how often it involves caddis flies. Even at its peak, there is a certain sense of dignity and order to the classic mayfly emergence, while caddis fly hatches are helter-skelter affairs, ranging from utter fizzle to the sort of uninhibited craziness on the Yellowstone that night. And when caddis are at their best, it just doesn't get any better.

Despite their significance to trout and trout fishermen, downwings suffer from a curious lack of respect, a phenomenon that says more about the way people think about fly fishing nowadays than it does about the way they actually fish. Name three species of caddis flies important to trout. Don't worry, I can't either. The fact is, you don't need to be an entomologist to catch lots of fish on caddis imitations, at least if you're smart enough or lucky enough to be in the right place at the right time. My sweetened condensed version of caddis lore is an exercise in simplicity: There are adults and pupae and larvae. There are big ones and little ones, brown ones and gray ones and tan ones, and that's about it. For practical purposes, even this limited fund of knowledge will get you through a lot of caddis hatches. Some people are evidently put off by this lack of scientific precision, but then they're usually the same people who spend their stream time worrying about the stock market. Personally, I prefer the hog-in-garbage model of good fortune when I'm lucky enough to stumble upon a genuinely insane caddis eruption, but that's just the kind of guy I am.

This edition of the caddis fly phenomenon involved a tan #14 something that my buoyant deer-hair version imitated quite well, which was just fine for a number of reasons. I was well stocked with the right fly, since the hide of one whitetail buck will produce about a million caddis fly imitations, and tying them appeals to the use-every-scrap ethic I bring to the chase each archery season. Furthermore, deer-hair patterns are durable under stress, an important consideration in wild-paced fishing like this, when time is finite and better spent catching fish than fumbling in fly boxes for replacements. Finally, deer-hair caddis are easy to see, an important consideration in big water like the Yellowstone, especially in failing light.

Darkness and the trauma of landing all those fish finally caught up with my deer-hair pattern, however. A close-range inspection against the sunset showed it to be mauled and battered beyond recognition, and even though this didn't seem to bother the fish any, it bothered me. I clipped off the tattered remnant and plucked a Royal Trude from one of my fly boxes. This pattern resembles a caddis fly in outline alone, but it is a wonderful floater, highly visible, and an old Yellowstone River standard for good reason, as Dick was proving a few yards downstream in the riffle. Now all I had to do was attach it to the end of my leader.

Like all lucky boys, I grew up thinking my father was infallible, especially in the outdoors, where he seemed to catch every fish he cast to, hit every grouse he shot at, and enjoy a vast and mysterious body of wisdom concerning everything we saw and did together in the field. My first indication that this infallibility might be more perceived than real came one night as we stood together somewhere casting to a pool full of rising trout. He needed to change flies for some reason, but he just couldn't do it. He held the tiny hook and the gossamer tippet at varying distances from his eyes, but nothing worked. Finally he asked me in a terse, controlled voice if I might spare a moment to tie the goddamn fly to the goddamn leader for him and I did. He was in his midforties then and I was in my early teens, and of course I just didn't understand. Now I had midforties visual problems of my own, and I suddenly understood his frustration perfectly well.

Darkness was seriously upon us. By holding the Trude and the end of the tippet up against the luminous riot of pinks and oranges in the western sky, I could identify the parts of the puzzle, but not their relationship. Needless to say, the crescendo of hungry trout noises and the constant patter of joyous expletives from Dick did nothing to calm the panic. I brought the fly up close, but my head only retreated re-flexively. I held everything out at arm's length, but the fly just disappeared. Finally I stabbed angrily at the hook eye with the end of the tippet until I managed to impale it purely by chance. I let go of the Trude and saw it hanging there from the strand of 5X with an overwhelming sense of relief.

The double slipknot may be archaic and inefficient in terms of breaking strength, but it can be tied reliably by feel—a critical consideration in ridiculous situations like this. One loop-over, two loop-overs, and one pull-through later I was fishing again, the Trude's bushy wing plainly visible against the reflected light from the river. If the sight of the fly on the water felt like a triumph, the strike that followed was its logical reward.

When you run into one of your buddies after an evening like this and he asks you how you did down on the river, saying "Well, I caught twenty-three fish between twelve and nineteen inches long" doesn't really convey as much information as saying "Man, it was utterly outrageous!" even though it seems as if it should. So I wasn't counting fish, and neither was Dick, but for a moment I almost wished that we had been, more as a tribute to the phenomenon than because we needed one of those pointless resumé entries. I really don't know how many fish we caught during the hour we stood there in the riffle, but it was a lot, so many that after awhile we stopped talking about it because there was nothing left to say. We just stood there, fishing relentlessly, casting into the dark well after the flies became invisible, and still we caught fish by feel and guesswork and the occasional random strike. If the moon had been full we might have stayed there all night, but finally I told Dick that I just couldn't stand it anymore. Evidently he couldn't either, because when I reeled up the last of the line and climbed back into the boat he did the same without protest.

The only remaining illumination came from the lights of town. We had a mile or so of water left before our takeout. The river was running proud and strong, and since the Yellowstone is one of the few Montana Blue Ribbon streams that can drown you with impunity, I felt a surge of anxiety as we pushed off into the current. There was really nothing to do but surrender to the power of the river. At one point we wound up in the middle of some vigorous standing waves with enough rise and fall to make us lose track of all the lights from town, but we got through it all right in the end. Then, finally, the takeout was there, and so was Annie and the truck, and it was over.

56

We were tired, and nobody said much as we loaded the boat onto the trailer for the short drive back upriver to Dick's house and cold beer. As I started to break down my fly rod, I paused under the streetlight and studied what was left of the Royal Trude. Nothing remained but a hook and a bedraggled puff of white hair, but the fly had died honorably in the line of duty, so I clipped it off and dropped it into my caddis box where, if nothing else, it might remind me of possibilities on days when the fish were laughing and nothing worthwhile seemed within reach.

For there will be such days; this much is certain. Some will come on this river, at this time of year, when we are doing just what we did that night. If I have learned anything over the years it is that peak experiences are seldom easily reproduced, and almost never as easily as writers would sometimes have you believe. But each time we try and fail, the sting of disappointment should be tempered by memories like these: of rivers that came alive just when we needed them to; of fly patterns that looked just right to the fish even if they didn't look just right to us; of secrets shared between fish and anglers as an indifferent world went about business of its own while we fished on into the darkest corners of the night.

Chapter 7

Road Trip

 *Divide, Montana.* It is my birthday, June 9. While birthdays don't warrant much celebration at this age, mine is a convenient reminder that the season of serious fishing is at hand. For weeks, giant stonefly nymphs of the genus *Pteronarcys* have been grumbling about on the bottom of the nearby Big Hole River, migrating toward its banks while they wait for their biological clocks to detonate. Soon the fabled salmon-fly hatch will begin. This event usually takes place the week of my birthday, which explains why we like to mark the occasion at streamside.

I have been fly fishing the Big Hole for forty years. I'm not really as old as that makes me sound, even now, with one more candle on the cake. My experience here derives not so much from longevity as from the fact that I have squandered a remarkably high percentage of my life adrift on Montana's rivers, which could be grounds for admiration or disapproval depending on one's regard for financial security, career advancement, and family values.

This year my birthday falls midweek, which means that the crowds have yet to descend upon the Big Hole in earnest. A dozen rigs line the stream access site just west of Divide, most appended by boat trailers. Their presence might dismay anyone naive enough to confuse this outing with a wilderness experience, but those familiar with the Big Hole in June know better.

We did not come here for solitude. There was plenty of that back home five hours' drive to the north, along with hot showers, soft beds, and some pretty damn good trout fishing as well. We left there last night for two reasons: because of the promise of truly big browns, the kind of trout that suck the air right out of your lungs as soon as you get one on the end of a fly line, and because of the primal impulse to see one's own hometown disappear in the rearview mirror. The need to hit the road can be nearly as compelling as the need to fish, and few places offer as many opportunities to satisfy both these urges as Montana.

The Big Hole is low and clear. Ordinarily, conditions like this are close to the fly fisher's heart, but now the serenity of the water flowing past fills me with vague apprehension. The Big Hole should be flexing its muscles for the salmon-flies, pushing its way up into the willows and offering those big browns a taste of their own color to disguise them in the shallows. The Big Hole has been plagued by summer de-watering for years, but now the culprit is poor mountain snowpack. The river is making me edgy, but there is finally nothing to do but pump up the rafts, slide them out into the current, and start fishing.

Nick is at the oars. The first mile of river is his birthday present to me, and I have every intention of taking advantage of his filial generosity. There are no duns in the air, so I reach for my nymph box. The fly shops up and down the Big Hole are full of uncanny *Pteronarcys* imitations, but I've always been more of an impressionist at the tying bench. My own woven stonefly nymphs sink like rocks and fool fish reliably, which is all that really matters. Besides, I feel better when I'm fishing with a fly that contains at least some material of my own harvest, and the wild turkey wing casings on my stonefly nymphs serve this ritual purpose admirably.

In the second raft, Ray and Joe pull for the opposite bank as I climb onto our forward seat and balance precariously against the lift and fall of the current. A western tanager flutters from its perch above the stream, an outrageous pixel of hot color against the monotonous green background of the willows. All that red and yellow seems so wonderfully unnecessary somehow, although doubtless the tanager might say the same of us.

Nick checks us adeptly a comfortable distance from the bank, but when I make the first cast of the trip, my spirits sink faster than the weighted nymph. The fly line's listless drift finally confirms what we should have known as soon as we saw the river. There isn't enough water. The hatch has fizzled. Happy goddamn birthday.

Fished with every spare ounce of enthusiasm I can muster, the first mile of river yields a handful of snags, an eight-inch rainbow, and a whitefish. This is when seasoned outdoor writers start going on about stoneflies, western tanagers, and The Meaning Of It All, but not me, not this time. We didn't drive five hours away from good fishing to listen to crap like that. A caddis hatch appears on the water. I row while Nick fishes an elk-hair dry. He catches two more small rainbows, but we didn't come for that either.

Nothing magical happens during the too-lazy trip downstream. The bugs and the hefty browns—the ones we really did come for—never appear. Evening shadows are sprawled all over the river by the time we finally reach the takeout at Melrose, at which point there is nothing left to do but haul the rafts up the bank and drive up to the nearest bar to enjoy two more staples of my annual birthday road trip: an NBA play-off game and cold beer.

No matter what the circumstances, the fishing on June 10 never seems genuine without a bit of a hangover.

Twin Bridges, Montana. And a bit of a hangover it is. Fortunately, we know just the cure for it.

Thomas Jefferson was without doubt one of our more cerebral presidents. When Lewis and Clark stood perplexed at the confluence of the Missouri's headwaters in 1805 and named this particular fork in honor of their patron, their choice resulted in a certain irony, at least to future generations of fly fishers, for the Jefferson is anything but a cerebral trout stream.

Broad-shouldered and brawling, the Jefferson gathers water from its more famous upstream relatives and conveys it across miles of rolling sage to the origin of the Missouri proper. While the journey is pleasant enough, the current runs through tight sweeping curves with deadwater on the inside and power to spare on the outside of each bend. And while the Jefferson is no place for fly fishing's more delicate rituals, it is a junk fisherman's dream.

The withering sun has already climbed above the mountains to the east by the time we ease the rafts down the bank and into the current. Ray and Joe lag behind, fiddling with their tackle. Nick balances in the bow while I prepare to sweat my sins away at the oars. He is rigged with an exquisitely nasty black Flashabugger, a definitive bigwater junk fly if ever there was one. We will begin by evoking Ray's own theory of exploration in unfamiliar water, which asserts that when trout holding in feeding positions are confronted by a properly presented Flashabugger or Egg-Sucking Leech, they *have* to react, whether by smashing the fly, short-striking, or fleeing in terror. Whatever the case, you will at least have enjoyed a look at them by the time you're done.

A hundred yards down the first bank, Nick's rod tip bucks suddenly. With the water low and clear and the sun high overhead, it's easy to identify the fish at once as a brown. It's big enough to warrant some attention, and I ease us over into the shallows against the opposite bank, where Nick soon has his fish at bay. A respectable nineteen inches or so in length, the fish sports rich golden flanks, a sullen countenance, and the porcine snout that characterizes brown trout once they get big enough to arouse real interest. What we need to do now is find this one's five-pound big brother.

For the rest of the morning the pace of the fishing remains steady, with browns rising up out of the clear green water just often enough to affirm a fisherman's version of the Protestant work ethic: Cast long enough, and your reward will come. They are almost all nice fish, but we just can't seem to cross the arbitrary threshold between nice fish and heart-stoppers.

Perhaps it's the indiscretion of the previous evening. Perhaps it's the relentless heat or the lassitude that settles upon us following our stream-side lunch. Whatever, we begin the afternoon fishing with muffled reflexes. Nick is subtly but distinctly goofing off at the oars. Unable to focus, I miss a fish that I should have hooked in the first run and, even more to the point, I don't really care. This is not the kind of attitude one needs when hunting large brown trout.

Then it happens. We float around a bend to find a flock of white pelicans assembled on the gravel bar ahead of us. The river carries us relentlessly closer until the birds take to the air together in a silent eruption of straining wings, like a white flower blooming in a time-lapse photographic sequence.

Transfixed by the pelicans, I am in the process of lifting the fly from the water to cast again when a stout shape the length of my forearm attacks it. Unable to check my own motion, I deftly snatch the streamer right out of the fish's maw. Suddenly aroused, I curse—at myself, not the fish—and roll another desperate cast into the same lie as the current sweeps us past. Amazingly, the huge fish rises from the depths a second time, but the Jefferson has us in its grip and we are gone before anything can come of it.

"Did you see that?" I ask Nick.

"See what?" he replies.

And so there are no witnesses in the end, just an empty spot in the water where the fish appeared with such tantalizing brevity to remind me of the river's bounty. Disappointed in myself, I suggest to Nick that we trade places and we pass awkwardly amidships, exchanging fly rod and oars in the process. Perched comfortably on the forward seat, he flicks the streamer against the bank like an expert. Nick looks confident, fit, and ready. Of course, he doesn't have a hangover, so comparisons are really unfair. Nonetheless, I can't help but feel the sudden momentum of the passing years.

Downstream, another long bank beckons. The trick is to put the loss of the fish behind you, to tell yourself that the rowing must be perfect, that nothing less will do. The second part of the trick is to believe it. Shoulders set against the oars, I ease into the rhythm of doing just that while Nick casts intently and the languid summer foliage that lines the Jefferson's banks slips by like an easy green dream.

I have seen the fish that we came for and understand the lesson of its loss. It is comforting to know what the river contains, even if it wasn't meant for me. There will be other days, other fish, and other rivers.

Livingston, Montana. Ray didn't want to leave the Jefferson, and every time I remember the fish that tried so hard to take my fly, I have to agree. Covering ground (and water) is an essential element of a good road trip, however, and seeing your friends is another. So here we all are, sprawled around the deck at the home of our friends Dick and Annie LeBlond, watching the Yellowstone surge past the eastern perimeter of their lawn and working on another version of earlier indiscretions as history seems destined to repeat itself.

There has been a change of characters. The boys have left for home and unsupervised adolescent mischief while Lori has driven down from home to meet us. That we are even looking at the Yellowstone in the second week of June confirms that this is an unusual year. The 'Stone should be blowing mud and challenging its banks, but the same scant snowpack that made the Big Hole such a disappointment has made the Yellowstone look promising indeed. Our rule of thumb is that when this river shows you some fishable water at this time of year, you had by-God better get busy and fish it.

Which is why I have let Ray talk me into one of his hysterical marathon floats. The plan is to put in right at Dick's house and fish our way downriver until the Yellowstone doesn't look like a trout stream anymore. Dick and Annie have to be in Big Timber for their son's baseball game, so we even get a free shuttle. As Ray himself puts it, we would be fools to decline an opportunity like this.

The following morning, the air is still cool as we haul the raft across Dick's lawn and lower it into the surging current. Ray is at the oars as we glide quietly through the sleepy remains of town. Casting from the stern, Lori hooks one whitefish after another on a stonefly nymph. Up front, I am working a Hare's Ear against the bank when the line hesitates and I set the hook into a sixteen-inch cutthroat. While the fish isn't the five-pound brown we have come for, anyone who cannot take time to appreciate a native cutthroat needs to reexamine his priorities. This one sports the rich yet subtle hues of burnished metal in its flanks that is the signature of the species here in the Yellowstone drainage. The namesake crimson markings along the leading edges of the gill covers look like botched vascular surgery. Accustomed to enjoying cutts in high, crystalline streams, I am always faintly amazed to find fish like this down at the edge of the prairie and the catfish water, but here one lies right in my hand, the definition of a pleasant surprise if ever there was one.

None of this writerly pap matters much to Ray, for whom big browns have become more of an obsession with each passing river mile. He begs off rowing and we trade positions in the raft. By the time I come up with both oars, he has a heavily weighted Bitch Creek nymph pitched against the bank and fished as deep as it will go. The technique is anything but subtle, but within a matter of minutes the line hisses back upstream and Ray is fast to a respectable fish that turns out to be the first brown of the day.

I hand my Big Ugly box back to Lori and spend the next several river miles dodging weighted nymphs and listening to the two of them howl at the moon as they hook one fish after another. There are more cutthroats, an occasional rainbow, and enough browns in the two-pound range to make it obvious that hooking the elusive hog is only a matter of time. A midriver Chinese fire drill finally leaves Lori at the oars, Ray in the stern, and me back astride the forward seat, my delicate little Hare's Ear replaced by a Bitch the size of my little finger. Unaccustomed to the physics of rafts in white water, Lori soon has us spinning backward downstream like a runaway top, but it is way too nice a day for her to take our criticism seriously.

Largely by accident, we eventually wind up in a small side channel lined by stately cottonwoods. The water settles down back in here as if it has taken a sedative, and the main river with its busy current and muscular standing waves soon recedes behind us. Here in the side channel the water is laced with shadows cast by the towering trees, and I can almost feel the presence of fish in the shallows adjacent to the banks.

Another cutthroat plucks my nymph from the bottom, and I am concentrating on getting the fish to the boat when I hear Ray set his hook in the stern. "There's one!" he cries, just as he has two dozen times already. Busy with a fish of my own, I pay no more attention until his reel screams and I hear him mumble in a subdued voice, "I'm going to need some help with this one."

Ray never needs help with much of anything, at least not with anything on the end of a fly line. Ignoring the cutthroat alongside the boat, I turn to discover Ray leaning precariously over the side with his rod bent double toward the water, where something large and substantial is pulsing back with raw authority. Lori is doing her best to check the raft against the current, but we are slowly moving away downstream and the fish is obviously not inclined to come with us.

Ray has always been an advocate of heavy leaders, and the rugged water of the Yellowstone scarcely demands anything subtle. I know he is rigged with a tippet adequate for steelhead or salmon, so his inability to budge the fish from its lie reflects size on the part of the fish rather than finesse on the part of the fisherman. Clearly, this is the one we have been after all along.

And then the contest is suddenly over. Nothing breaks; the hook simply slides free from an inadequate purchase inside the fish's mouth, leaving Ray holding nothing but slack line and disappointment. We accelerate downstream as if released from an anchor rope. "Aw, shit," Ray says gently to the river, and then there is nothing left to do but drift away from the scene of the encounter in numb silence, with the fish that caused all the excitement free to grow forever in the fertile waters of the imagination.

And there you have it: the road trip as an exploration of the inevitable, the feasible, and the merely possible. Birthdays come whether we want them to or not, and the road is there anytime we choose to take to it. Sometimes, however, we can only suppose what great trout streams hold for us; the actual getting must remain beyond our ken. Those are the possibilities that drive the world of outdoor sport. They propel us eagerly from the realm of the comfortable toward strange new horizons where pursuit is the order of the day and there is no such thing as a bad time, at least when viewed in the proper perspective.

As a matter of intellectual curiosity, it is worth asking what would have happened had we managed to land one of those bruisers. The answer, of course, is not much. There would have been some back-slapping and a picture or two, but nothing as final as elk antlers on the wall or a pheasant dinner. The river would have just as many fish as it does now and so would we. Does that make the whole exercise pointless? Perhaps, but no more pointless than anything else. It is the possibility of fish that we have come for rather than their possession.

And what would become of us without possibilities such as these?

Chapter 8

Days of the Locust

One hundred—the century mark. It can be a large number or a small one depending on the context. Years ago, when it approximated my lifetime Little League batting average, it was a very small number indeed, which is one reason why I abandoned team sports at an early age in favor of fly rods, bows, and shotguns.

On the other hand, when there are three figures flashing from the digital thermometer on the bank as I drive through my hometown on a summer afternoon, that represents a very large number indeed. When it gets that hot, the dry prairie air feels as if it can scorch your flesh, and no one in their right mind goes out in the sun unless they have to. On days like this, the choice is simple: sulk indoors or gird up your loins and fish hoppers.

Downstream from town, the air crackles and buzzes in the withering grip of summer as I pull to a stop on a friend's ranch and study the creek. The current is running as low and clear as I have ever seen it. Through my polarized glasses the water assumes a surreal, crystalline quality, almost as if it is not there at all. The details of the gravel bottom seem impossibly distinct, and the aquatic vegetation glows like shattered emeralds in the sun. Combines are running through a wheat field above the creek to the southwest, and a hot wind is kicking up from the same direction. It is the addition of the wind that promises to make the afternoon perfect, for reasons we shall soon explore.

Down at the first pool, I wade right in wearing nothing but cut-off jeans and old running shoes. The creek's cool presence teases its way up my legs and finally grabs at my crotch, and for a moment there is nothing to do but gasp in shock and get used to it. Tension eases as my physiology adjusts to its new environment, and suddenly I am more comfortable than I have been all day.

The combination of wind, light tackle, and bulky flies raises obvious technical concerns, but the breeze is at my back for the most part as I work the line out against the opposite bank, and I don't mind a little *splat* when a hopper pattern hits the water anyway. Still, I'm having trouble getting the leader to turn over crisply with all that mass on the end, which is causing drag problems in the complex crosscurrents, and then, what the hell, the fly disappears from the surface in a slurping rise anyway.

In creeks like this one, hot weather always seems to mean hot fish, and this particular eighteen-inch 'bow turns out to be about all I can handle. At first it jumps high and hard as if the water has somehow become a source of pain that must be escaped. When it finally settles into the business of running around the pool, each change of direction is marked by a sharp metallic flash down in the current's cool green belly. Then the fish is off downstream, but something happens on the way through the first riffle, leaving me with nothing but a flaccid length of fly line and the rest of the afternoon in which to replace the naked energy the fish took from me when it left.

And what an afternoon it proves to be. Browns. Rainbows. My God. We associate large surface flies in clear water with slashing rises, but not today. Often the fly just disappears, as it did to the first fish. Then the browns start doing their special hopper trick—appearing inches beneath the fly and following it languidly downstream longer than you can imagine possible. Since a good number of these are *big* browns, the suspense is enough to get me twitching and talking to the fish (Take it! Take it, you son of a bitch!). Over the years I've learned that if I actually talk to the fish for more than an hour or so at a time, I really ought to give it up for awhile. Finally one last brown breaks me off and I do just that.

As I reel in the line and climb up the bank and head back toward the truck, I remind myself to watch carefully for snakes now that I am back on dry land, since snakes thrive in this kind of weather every bit as much as hoppers do. I run into a rattler or two down here every year during hopper season. I've spent enough time in snake country to know how badly rattlesnakes want to avoid biting you, but that is a hard notion to keep in mind when you've got one of those thick-as-your-arm prairie dragons coiled up and buzzing next to your foot.

I did have one hit me once. I happened to be wearing heavy waders that day. The snake was small and it bounced right off my boot, which no doubt saved me a whole lot of trouble. I wore waders faithfully for the rest of the season, but then one day it got so hot that I decided I would rather take my chances with the snakes, and I've never gone back. At this time of year the pleasures of wading wet are just too sublime to deny. I figure I've made my peace with the snakes. So far, so good.

Back at the truck, I break down the rod and lay it across the dash. This is not the approved means of transporting a fine fly rod, but I'm back and forth to the creek so much this time of year that I just can't make myself take time to store it properly. This compromise to expediency may cost me someday, just the way going bootless in snake country may cost me, but I've made an executive decision to accept these risks as the cost of doing what I love to do the way I love to do it.

The creek still looks tempting, but I know when to quit. There are dogs to train, bows to shoot, kids who deserve my attention.

Besides, there is also tomorrow.

Man has always had an uneasy relationship with members of the order Orthoptera. To Aesop, the grasshopper provided a symbol of dissipation to contrast with the industrious ant. In Old Testament terms, locusts were a definitive form of divine retribution, God's own equivalent of a stick up alongside the head. Here in Montana farm country, grasshoppers are still about as popular as hail and taxes. But in this age of biopolitical correctness we are supposed to be able to find something to love about even the most unlovable species. In the case of the grasshopper, this is easier if you have a fly rod in your hand.

There are some things you need to know about fishing hoppers, but arcane details of insect taxonomy are not among them. This is a diverse bunch of bugs to be sure, but understanding the factors that get trout cued in to hoppers is far more important than precise imitation of particular species. Knowing that there are big hoppers and little hoppers is really about as far as you need to take it, and I could fish hoppers happily all summer with a single pattern on a #8 hook. The grass may be full of much smaller specimens, but those are usually immature forms that don't do what hoppers have to do to provoke excitement from hungry trout. The fish don't pay much attention to the little guys, so I don't either.

Weather is important. Heat is one major variable, as we have already seen. Hot, dry weather is trophic to grasshoppers the way rain is trophic to inbound steelhead. Scorching days are what make grasshoppers grow and jump and otherwise behave in ways that make them interesting to fish. That and the insects' natural rate of maturation explain why I seldom get serious about fishing hoppers until late July, and regard the dog days of August as prime hopper season.

The other critical weather factors are wind and humidity. In contrast to mays, caddis, and other aquatics, hoppers arrive in trout streams purely by accident. Adept jumpers that they are, they seldom make a significant appearance in streams without a bit of wind drift to scramble their guidance systems. Moisture, on the other hand, tends to suppress hoppers by making them less active and promoting the growth of debilitating fungus on their wings. All of which explains why hot, dry, windy summer days are so dear to the Montana trout-fisher's heart.

For the effectiveness of hopper imitations depends above all else on the presence of naturals in the water. There doesn't have to be a lot of them, but there must be a few, enough for the fish to move up out of the holes and into the shallows against the banks. Bear in mind that this is ordinarily the *least* attractive part of a trout stream to a trout on a bright sunny day. Fish are vulnerable there to all sorts of predators and they know it. In other words, it takes hoppers to coax trout into hopper water.

Of course, fishing that water requires nothing less than a willing suspension of disbelief. *There?* the newcomer to hopper fishing usually begins by asking. *You want me to cast there?* Such skepticism is understandable. Good hopper water is often shallow and unprotected. Although you can usually count the pebbles on the bottom, you almost never see fish unless they are actively feeding, even when they are there. The only real requirements for classic hopper water are that it be wet and close to a grassy bank, and to the uninitiated much of the best of it looks as if it should belong in the *you gotta be kidding* category.

Well, I'm not. It's impossible to present a hopper pattern too closely to the bank. As a matter of fact, bouncing one right off the grass and into the water is a classy little exercise in finesse that is well worth the effort when fishing to sophisticated fish. I prefer to cast across current rather than work the bank ahead of me, because I spook fewer fish that way. Of course, in faster water this approach often requires desperate and furious line mending, especially when casting a bulky fly in windy conditions with the light tippets often needed during typical summer conditions of bright light and low, clear water. The central point is this: You must make yourself fish that water no matter how much it reminds you of casting into a dry martini. Otherwise you're just not hopper fishing.

You can learn a lot about this business by catching yourself a hatful of hoppers, pitching them into some likely looking run, and watching what happens. One of my favorite places to indulge in such pseudoscientific pleasures is from an old irrigation pipe that crosses my home stream just above a long stretch of classic hopper water. One thing I've learned there is that if I can watch a live hopper float all the way down that bank and around the next bend undisturbed, I had better find something else to do because the fish aren't hitting hoppers.

On the positive side, it's worth noting what a tremendous amount of disturbance hoppers create on the water. Let's face it: They are not glad to be there and they act accordingly. Fish often seem to key on the hopper's graceless arrival and frantic attempts to extricate itself from the mess it's gotten itself into, which is why I'm not above slapping an imitation onto the water and giving it a little action once it's there. Such tactics have turned more than one day around for me.

It's also worth noting that grasshoppers are lousy swimmers, which should come as no surprise. Their heavy, chitinous exoskeletons are designed to serve them well on land, not at sea. In fact, after an initial period of struggle, hoppers usually sink like stones, which leads to another tactical recommendation: Don't hesitate to fish hopper patterns wet.

I know, I know. The whole point of this is to catch big fish on dry flies, but you still do what you gotta do. And what I do if I start to get short strikes on dry hopper patterns is to let them drown and keep on fishing. Under typical bright conditions, it's usually an easy matter to follow large hopper patterns visually even underwater, so the aesthetics of the strike don't really change much, except that sometimes they come a lot more frequently.

Ranging easily from the sublime to the ridiculous, hopper patterns themselves are a fine testimonial to the Impressionist School of Fly

Tying. Old standbys like Joe's Hopper work. Modern masterpieces of the fly tyer's art that look like science fair projects work. Well-greased Muddler Minnows work. (Muddlers look at least as much like grasshoppers as they do like the sculpins they are supposed to represent, which should tell us something about the literal veracity of the whole business of imitative fly tying.) I've never been able to appreciate much difference among these options, and my daughter Jenny was tying perfectly functional hopper imitations when she was seven years old. After a fish or two, they all look like something you would scrape off your windshield anyway.

The fact is, trout cued in to hoppers are usually ready to hit almost anything that remotely looks like one, and if they don't, the fault usually lies with the presentation rather than the pattern. Other than going up or down a hook size from time to time I don't think any of this matters much. My personal standard is a bushy, buggy model with a yellow deer hair body, pheasant rump feather legs (sort of), wild turkey quill wings, and a natural deer hair head and overwing on a Tiemco 2302 2X long fine wire hook. I'm only partial to this version because I like the way it floats and I enjoy the fact that I can collect all the materials myself.

Except for the hook.

Of course these attempts at definition should not disguise the fact that hopper patterns are sometimes a handy solution to fishing's little problems even when there is no compelling reason for them to be.

One fine August day I was on my way back from somewhere when I found myself on the upper Missouri with several hours to kill before heading home. Despite the size and number of fish this water contains, it has never been a personal favorite. For my money, the upper Missouri suffers from all the nose-picky qualities of spring creek fishing without any of the intimacy or charm, an opinion with which others are welcome to disagree, as a great many evidently do.

From my vantage high above the river, I could appreciate an eyeful of typical Montana summer scenery: sagebrush shimmering in the heat, plains turned brown from lack of moisture, the occasional dimple of a feeding fish on the lazy water below, and a scattering of rather worried looking fly fishers distributed up and down the banks of the river. The anglers seemed well appointed and intent, but most weren't even casting, and no one seemed remotely close to catching any fish.

I sat down and ate a sandwich and watched, and during this period of observation concluded that if none of these studious types had figured out what the fish were rising to, I probably wasn't going to either. Finally I assembled my rod and walked down to an unobtrusive spot beside a long, monotonous stretch of water and tied on one of my standard deer-hair-whatever hopper patterns.

The fly hit the water like a wounded bird, but before it floated the length of the rod it disappeared into a slurping rise and I was fast to a typical Missouri rainbow: bright, bullet shaped, hot as a shotgun barrel at the end of an early season dove shoot. The fish roared in and out of the weed beds so many times I thought I would never see it again, but somehow it wound up next to me along the bank where I fought it to a standstill and released it. Remember that I never said anything derogatory about the *fish* in the Missouri.

Actually, I caught several more before I decided to call it a fishing trip and get on down the line toward home. I drew a few stares as I walked up the bank to the truck. Out in the current, fish were still rising sporadically to something and people were still failing to catch them despite painfully serious attempts to do so. No one actually said anything to me as I left. It was probably better that way.

Everyone knows that all the really big trout live out here, in Montana, where a river runs through everything and fly fishing is a virtual way of life. Everyone knows that these fish spend most of their time feeding on subsurface pork chop equivalents like giant stonefly nymphs and sculpins. Everyone knows that there are only a few opportunities to take such fish up top, and that those hatches are the stuff of fly-fishing legend. *Pteronarcys californica. Ephemerella grandis. Xanthippus corallipes.*

Whoa there, you say. Run option three by one more time!

All right. I admit that fishing hoppers lacks something of the élan common to those other storied events, but therein lies the charm. Good hopper water can be found in obscure places, and is best fished after the crowds are gone. I can spend a whole weekend in August taking big fish on hoppers and run into fewer people than I'd see in the parking lot at a popular stream access site on Blue Ribbon water during the salmon-fly hatch. Often, it's just me and the cows and the snakes and the sun. And the fish, of course. Let's not forget the fish.

Despite their problems, hopper patterns are fun to tie and fun to fish. Factor in high-visibility strikes, teasing follows, and the appeal of big browns acting uncharacteristically gullible, and it's easy to understand the faraway look some of us get out here when the mercury climbs and the wind kicks up and the summer sun beats down relentlessly on the high plains.

It's a different kind of fishing to be sure, without the measured cadence of a mayfly hatch or the subtleties of tiny emergers hung delicately in the film. For those who measure their streamside experiences by such refined standards, the days of the locust may call for some attitude adjustment. Hit it right, though, and you will find a way to adjust.

Believe me.

Chapter 9

Stupid Flies,
Smart Trout

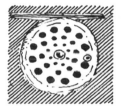 Montana spring creeks hold their share of secrets, but the presence or absence of feeding trout is seldom one of them. Because of the clarity and delicacy of these waters, experienced hands can usually determine at a glance whether the switch that tells flies to hatch and trout to feed is in the on position or not. If it isn't, it *really* isn't, and on this particular late-spring day I had no trouble determining that it was not. Blue-winged olives should have been coming off the creek, but the swallows were a thousand feet overhead and the airspace above the water was utterly devoid of bugs.

I hiked up the bank to an overlook from which I could study one of my favorite feeding riffles and confirmed the obvious. There was no hatch and there wasn't a trout in sight. It was hard to reconcile the stream's vacant appearance with how that same riffle looked yesterday as the surface churned with activity and feeding fish. Now I faced a dilemma. I could tie on a representative of the insect that was supposed to be emerging and fish blindly, a nearly certain exercise in futility. I could sit on the bank and bird-watch and contemplate the General Theory of Relativity until something started to happen down there in the creek. I could go home and devote the day to tying flies or training retrievers or some other socially worthwhile project. Or I could fish junk and try to catch some trout.

When the going gets tough, the tough go fishing. I trudged on up the bank to a spot where the creek gathers itself in a coil like a snake poised to strike. There the current's velocity has carved a hidden channel into the bottom. That in turn made me feel ever so slightly less ridiculous as I prepared to cast blindly into the run. As I studied the slot of deep water, I rummaged through the darkest corners of my vest for the fly boxes one seldom exposes in polite company. Finally my hand closed on my Junk Box as if it were contraband. It was time for (shudder) a San Juan Worm.

Never mind the propriety of all this; we can debate that later. Let's also agree not to imagine the feel of such a fly when cast by a delicate three-weight rod or the inglorious *plop* it makes upon impact with that pristine water. Let us instead allow our imagination to leap ahead to my fourth cast, when the line hesitated and the rod tip bounced and the eighteen-inch rainbow erupted from the bottom of the pool and tail-walked across the riffle below it, disappearing around the bend with a pleasantly amazed angler in furious pursuit. That will probably make the rest of this narrative easier on all of us.

I did land that fish, after an unusual amount of up-and-down-the-bank aerobics even by the standards of nice 'bows on light tackle. I landed the next two or three as well, and then I struck too hard and lost my SJW to a sullen brown right at the top of the run. Then it was time to dip into the Junk Box for more ammo.

This business went on for nearly an hour and a half until, frankly, I couldn't stand it any longer. The hatch never materialized, but I didn't really care, not after all those fish. Back in town, I stopped to gas up the truck and ran into another local fisherman, a guy I like too much to lie to even though I don't really enjoy sharing secrets with him. He didn't have to ask if I had been fishing.

"What's going on down at the creek?" he asked casually.

"Not a damn thing," I replied.

"Cold front musta put the hatches off," he suggested.

"Didn't see a fish rise all afternoon," I assured him, as I silently congratulated myself for avoiding this outstanding opportunity to compromise the truth.

Is there anything as uplifting as a clean conscience?

I admit that I have something of an ambivalent relationship with spring creeks. I happen to live next to a good one, which I fish an awful lot, even though I'm within easy shooting distance of many of the nation's best-known trout streams. Even so, when I'm off fishing the Madison or the Big Hole or the Yellowstone, it's hard to keep from wondering what's going on back home. Spring creeks do that to you, demanding your time and attention like jealous lovers.

On the other hand, it's hard for those of the modern American fly-fishing movement's trout-bum wing not to view some spring creek fishing with a certain uneasiness. Many better-known spring creeks are home to lots of the style-over-substance goings-on that drive me crazy, the substance (lest we forget) being catching fish on flies. And then there is the fact that spring creeks can be technically tough to the point of humiliation. To be honest, they're sometimes too tough for me, although that's at least part of their loopy charm.

One of the quirkiest aspects of the Montana spring creek character is the on-or-off quality of the fishing, especially since *off* means *off* the way *no* means *no*. It is perfectly possible, say, to spend a wonderful day fishing a steelhead stream that contains absolutely no steelhead, this paradox made possible because typical steelhead water is just too polite to let you know when it is barren. Ignorance really *can* be a form of bliss. By their very nature, spring creeks allow no such suspension of disbelief. What you see is what you get, and if the creek is quiet the fishing probably will be too.

So. You're there and it isn't happening. You can go home, become a philosopher, or fish junk.

The notion of opening my Junk Box in such a rarefied atmosphere was first thrust upon me years ago as I was preparing for a day on one of Montana's better-known spring creeks. Back then, the idea of paying actual money to go spend a day fishing in someone's backyard seemed vaguely unsettling to me (and to tell you the truth, it still does). But a friend knew the owner, and our visit was billed as an informal affair, which made it an offer I couldn't refuse. Feeling a bit intimidated, I called another friend who had fished the place before to ask his advice about fly patterns.

"#2 Woolly Buggers," he responded without hesitation.

"*What?*" I screamed indignantly into the telephone.

"I mean it," he said. "There's some real hogs in there. You can stand around trying to match the hatch and catch sixteen-inchers if you want to, but I'd rather strap on some junk and catch big fish."

To tell you the truth, I didn't really have the courage to test his theory, although mutual friends assure me they've seen him land numerous fish over five pounds in that creek using just such methods.

Let's define some terms. By junk, I don't necessarily mean #2 Woolly Buggers (although I don't necessarily *not* mean #2 Woolly Buggers). Let's simply refer to the use of flies not specifically intended to represent any identifiable insect on or about the water, remembering that matching the hatch is by most accounts the essence of the Spring Creek Experience.

Accordingly, the most important junk fly in my spring creek armamentarium is the #16 Bead-Head Hare's Ear. The beauty of this omnipotential nymph pattern is that it looks enough like so many things that there is always a statistically acceptable possibility a trout will mistake it for something, even if the trout is a highly selective and world-wise spring creek veteran. The Hare's Ear was always my basic exploratory pattern on my home water, a role for which the addition of a bead head made it even more admirably suited. Over the years, I have undoubtedly taken more fish with some variation on this theme than with all specific patterns combined. Run into me out there with one on the end of the tippet and I could tell you I'm fishing the nymphal form of Such and Such, but this probably would be stretching matters. More likely, I just don't know what the hell is going on and I'm doing my best to catch some fish anyway.

It doesn't really seem fair to classify hopper patterns as junk. As we have already seen, deer-hair and turkey-quill bugs really can match hatches, albeit ones that occurred some distance from the stream. But out in this country, hopper patterns can always be used to liven up still waters, and perfectly reasonable hopper imitations can degenerate into junk of the lowest order no matter how legitimate the intention of their original design.

One fine summer morning on my way home from somewhere, I stopped along a little high-plains stream known to almost no one but a few locals who prize its undiscovered population of big browns. The water never looks like much, which is probably why so many people drive right by it, but on this particular day, after a long, dry summer and lots of irrigation, the stream looked frankly pathetic. What current remained had contracted into a few shallow channels that didn't have enough energy to be called riffles, and the only water that could possibly hold fish worth catching lay in sluggish runs along undercut banks choked with willows. If you didn't know better, you would have trouble imagining four-pound catfish there, much less four-pound browns. But I did know better.

This stream doesn't support much insect life to begin with, and by the time I rigged up and climbed down the bank, it was apparent that civilized fishing as we know it was out of the question. With a nervous glance over my shoulder, I fumbled through the darkest recesses of my vest in search of the obvious solution to the problem confronting me: a Grayback.

Vintage Montana junk, the Grayback is a simple pattern (a yellow chenille body with deer hair on top and soft grizzly hackle in front) born and bred in the same blue-collar company as Big Horn Specials, Goofus Bugs, and the like. Originally conceived as a hopper imitation, it can still pass muster as such, although the chenille body's tendency to waterlog makes it a frustrating pattern to fish on the surface. The Grayback really comes into its own when fished wet deliberately, especially when presented downstream. Remember: No one ever said this was going to be pretty—or even civilized.

Abandoning all principles of good taste, I tied one on, slogged out into the tepid current, and positioned myself upstream from a deep hole carved out of the opposite bank. The brush made a proper quartering cast impossible, so finally I gave up, moved farther out into the stream, and let the Grayback wash down into the deep water where it hung in the current like some kind of tethered vermin. I tried to imagine ways in which this differed from fishing for carp with doughballs, but couldn't come up with anything convincing. Then an angry boil appeared at the end of my leader, and the rod leapt as a fish smashed the fly and retreated back into the security of the willows.

The excitement didn't last long. Large trout, light leaders, and water choked with brush are an inherently unstable combination, and I was soon reeling in my line minus both fish and fly. I managed one good look at the brown down there in its lair before we parted company, however, and it was a big one. Was this really fly fishing? I wondered as I waded back to the bank to collect my composure. Was this something I would be proud to have my children see me doing? Did that brown trout really weigh four pounds?

Who cares? I gleefully answered to all three questions as I rummaged through my Junk Box and headed downstream to the next hole. Some days, that's just the kind of attitude you need if you're going to advance the cause of angling.

Of course junk flies reach an apotheosis of sorts in the form of the San Juan Worm, which is sort of an ultimate fly fisher's Stupid Pet Trick. Even avowed nihilists like me are likely to place a discreet hand across the hook holder (sort of like a fig leaf) when it contains a fly like that, especially when accosted by polite company on delicate waters. And just because I admit to fishing SJWs from time to time myself doesn't mean I'd want my daughter to marry someone who did.

But then there are times when you do what works and say the hell with the rest. On my home stream, SJWs are dynamite early in the season when spring rain has added a touch of color to the current and swept a few naturals into the runs along the banks. Since these kinds of conditions often put more politically correct insect activity out of sync, you might even argue that under such circumstances you really *are* matching the hatch. Or you can simply enjoy the fish as they come along and find topics for conversation other than fly selection should friends with taste and manners appear at streamside.

Of course, junk flies on delicate water pose a number of problems, both practical and aesthetic.

Most spring creek tackle is poorly suited to handling bulk and weight. My own standard three-weight is hardly a first choice when it comes to driving a heavy fly crosswind with anything like accurate placement, but somehow it always gets the job done. And there is no law against having a more substantial outfit back in the truck should circumstances warrant.

On a more serious note, it's worth remembering that junk flies can be hard on fish. Trout quite capable of putting up with a season's worth of fun and games on #18s need some extra TLC when taken on larger patterns. An argument against junk flies on pristine waters? No. An argument for barbless hooks and careful release technique.

And then there is the more subjective issue of propriety, the should-we-be-doing-this question that my instincts tell me to leave to others while we go fishing. Obviously, delicate technique and cognitive challenges are part of both the lure and the charm of Montana spring creeks, and the methods under discussion may well suggest to some a violation of these principles. Turning to *reductio ad absurdum*, should we remove all streamers from our trout vests, recall the Muddler Minnow, boycott the manufacturers of long-shanked hooks? Just as there is indeed a time for style, there is a time for substance, a fact worth remembering no matter where or with whom one is fishing.

It is seven o'clock on a muggy, lightly overcast, absolutely wonderful June evening. We have spent the day on the Beaverhead. I always head this way at some point during Montana's annual giant stonefly hatch because the Beaverhead doesn't have any giant stoneflies, an exercise in illogic that speaks volumes about both the politics of trout fishing and my own personality.

We have spent a long day playing Pac Man in the rafts, weaving our way among rocks and flicking flies of all descriptions into the willows that line the Beaverhead's banks like insulation around a water pipe. It was hard work at the oars, and I lost days' worth of output from the tying bench to the willows, but there were plenty of big browns and now we are all lounging around camp in a state of near total satiety.

But not quite. I've still got a fish or two left in me, and so do Ray and the kids. Since the Beaverhead fishes poorly from shore and we have neither the time nor the energy to set up another float, we pile into Ray's truck and head for Poindexter Slough.

A confession: Poindexter Slough is the kind of water that gives me a headache, especially after a riotous, pedal-to-the-metal day on a river like the Beaverhead. A delicate, clear water fish factory, its canny resident trout flee like spooked antelope as soon as a head appears above the bank, and casting to a feeding fish twice there without sending it into the weed beds qualifies as a brilliant personal success.

There are cars in the parking area, and the banks of Poindexter Slough contain a scattering of the usual suspects. Most everyone seems to be standing around looking, like spectators at an art opening uncertain as to how they should react to the stuff on the wall. Occasionally someone manages a tentative cast. All this is way too refined for my tastes, and it occurs to me that we could be back in camp drinking beer.

Ray and the boys and I walk upstream and approach the bank cautiously, as if we might be jump-shooting ducks. There are fish feeding in the pool below us and I am trying to get a fix on the bugs in the air.

Joe and Nick, now aged ten, are getting restless. Finally, Joe breaks the silence. "Dad," he asks Ray. "Do you think a Woolly Bugger would work?"

Of course this suggestion is just what we need to rescue the evening from terminal stuffiness. Hell yes, we tell him. Go get 'em. And he does.

Over the next several minutes, the following sequence of events takes place in and about the waters of Poindexter Slough. Boy casts Woolly Bugger. Fly hits water. Three-pound trout hits fly. Boy falls into Slough. Commotion attracts discreet observers from upstream and down. Boy lands and releases trout. Ray and I agree that there is nothing more Poindexter Slough can possibly offer us tonight, so we retreat in the direction of camp and refreshments.

"That looked like a pretty good fish," one of the bystanders comments as we walk back along the bank. This is obviously meant to be the beginning of a conversation in which useful information is exchanged.

"Sure was," I reply noncommittally. He wants me to tell him more. He wants me to tell him how a ten-year-old kid pulled off a stunt like that, and he especially wants me to tell him what fly he used to do it. "Look," I finally tell him. "It's better if you don't ask."

And no doubt it is.

There has always been an odd distinction in the approach to fly patterns taken by western fly fishers compared with their more traditional eastern counterparts. Historically, most advances in the science of imitative fly fishing evolved east of the Mississippi, perhaps because heavily fished eastern trout were more sophisticated consumers, and perhaps because the character of eastern fishing gives eastern fishermen a lot more time to squander at the tying bench.

Montanans, on the other hand, have always taken a more in-your-face attitude toward their fly patterns, with boundless enthusiasm for large attractors and buoyant, bushy dries. As Montana trout guru Dan Bailey once put it, a selective western trout is one that won't hit a Royal Wulff. That pronouncement certainly sounds dated now, but it still illustrates an important historical difference in philosophy. Out here, goofy flies enjoy a tradition every bit as secure as that of the Light Cahill and Quill Gordon on eastern waters.

Modern fly-fishing literature has largely ignored these over-the-top patterns, which is a shame given the amount of simple pleasure provided by Graybacks and Woolly Worms and whatnot. And it's worth remembering that these flies have endured for the most elementary reason of all: They catch fish. Even smart trout enjoy guilty pleasures once in awhile, and there is no reason why smart anglers shouldn't too.

Let's just hope that no one we know catches us in the act, unless they've got Junk Boxes of their own hidden away in the bottom of their vests.

Chapter 10

Big Bugs

 As is the case with many legendary experiences, the salmon-fly hatch can be the subject of great misconception. For the experienced fly fisher unfamiliar with the western waters where this phenomenon takes place, it can be almost impossible to get an accurate reading on what goes on out here in June. Should you fall into this category, it may help if you realize that many locals share your sense of confusion about this event. As is usually the case, your final expectations all depend on which sources of information you choose to believe.

There are enthusiasts who will tell you that during The Hatch you should *plan* on catching five-pound trout until your arms ache. If only it were so. Outdoor writers and fishing guides have not done nearly enough to dispel this notion, which at best has a tangential relationship to what actually goes on at streamside.

There are relative realists who will tell you that, whatever else it may be, The Hatch is the best time, if not actually the only time, to catch big Montana trout on dry flies. While less fabulous than the preceding view, this is still a somewhat less than accurate assessment of events.

And then there are the outright cynics, who will take great pains to tell you that The Hatch is pure hype, a media-inspired circus, the absolute worst time of the year to be caught on one of Montana's Blue Ribbon trout streams. It can be discouraging to note how many of these naysayers live close to the geographic heart of the phenomenon, which should provide a clue as to just how elusive and frustrating the salmon-fly hatch actually turns out to be. Fortunately for all concerned, most such sweeping condemnations also happen to be untrue. By and large.

I should confess at the outset that I myself have belonged to all three of the above camps at various times. For that matter, I have ascribed to all three points of view during the same week, and will probably do so again before the end of next June. There have been days when I changed my mind about The Hatch five different times on one float trip down the Big Hole. I share this sense of uncertainty to help you appreciate just how difficult it is to get a fix on the salmon-fly experience.

But I'm still there every year, like a swallow at Capistrano. It can't be because of the hype; I'm immune to that by now. It isn't just the fish. I have plenty of them close to home, in waters too small for salmon-flies and their attendant hassles. Let's face it. There is a certain mystique associated with this hatch, a sense that the whole is somehow greater than the sum of the parts. And mystique is something that a writer can sink his teeth into, especially if the sinking involves going fishing. So let us do just that, and try to discover together what it is that makes ordinarily wise anglers and canny trout begin each summer here in Montana by acting like fools, albeit happy ones.

The Bugs

Pteronarcys californica. There. I said it. You can't write a fly-fishing story nowadays without offering the scientific name for something, and I would just as soon discharge this conventional obligation at the earliest opportunity.

In fact, even among the duly esteemed blue-winged olives, green drakes, and pale morning duns, no other insect dominates a fishing experience quite the way this one does. Part of the big bugs' appeal stems from the very fact that you don't need collecting screens and magnifying glasses and reference books and two years of Latin to appreciate their emergence and what it means to you or the fish. Now that you're here, you can follow local custom and call them salmon-flies (although they have nothing to do with salmon) or, in their nymphal stage, hellgrammites (even though this term technically refers to dobson fly larvae). You can call them willow flies or giant stones and still be understood. In Ennis or Livingston or a dozen other strategically located Montana communities, at the right time of year you can just call them Bugs and everyone will know what you're talking about. I for one find this simplicity refreshing, and it seems that a lot of other people do, too.

The giant stonefly is a fascinating beast indeed. Turn over a rock and scoop up one of those big, black nymphs. Let it crawl up and down your arm for awhile. After a minute or so you'll be ready to give it a name, take it home to the kids, and build it a kennel in back of the garage. Can any other insect in a trout's diet inspire this kind of fascination?

After spending the winter wiggling around the stream bottom, salmon-fly nymphs begin to move toward the banks, where they eventually emerge as adults. This migration is the subject of intense scrutiny and speculation. Early each summer, one can observe previously sane people wading into rivers like the Madison or the Big Hole, grubbing among the rocks, and emerging from the holy waters muttering things like "End of the week, maybe," or "I've never seen 'em so late." This is a certain cultural signal that the annual circus involving trout, anglers, and *P. californica* is about to begin again.

The actual emergence of the duns brings all these involved parties into a sort of communal frenzy. The bugs don't just appear, the way mayflies and caddis do. The Hatch takes place in a more or less predictable march upstream, with the leading edge advancing at a rate of several miles per day. This apparent sense of order leads to still more evidence-gathering and prognostication by the faithful, who instead of turning over rocks in the stream will now be found racing up- and downriver scanning the skies and examining willow branches as if they contain the key to the secrets of the universe. And then it will only be a matter of time until you overhear such statements as "The flies are above the lake!" and "They're all the way to Yankee Jim!"—as if these pronouncements really do explain matters of cosmic significance.

The object of all this attention certainly is quite a bug. The adult salmon-fly's bulk exceeds that of a typical mayfly by several orders of magnitude, which no doubt explains much of its appeal to fish and fishermen alike. As noted, its identification scarcely requires a degree in invertebrate biology. Folks who cannot tell a caddis fly from a bumblebee have no trouble identifying giant stones in the air at considerable distances. There is something operatic about the salmon-flies' eventual return to the stream that bore them, when the huge duns descend from the sky with their great wings fluttering. Despite this apparent effort, the flies lose altitude relentlessly, like airplanes that have fallen behind the power curve, until they crash loudly upon the water. Follow one's course downstream far enough and you will probably see it disappear into some trout's mouth, at which point you will know that nature has been served once again.

One gathers at times that the flies themselves are half the fun. All true enthusiasts are expected to eat one themselves from time to time, an exercise in silliness I admit to participating in once although I don't necessarily recommend it. This took place at the end of a long day, and yes, beer was being consumed, and no, it (the salmon-fly) didn't taste very good. Even so, it's hard to imagine a ritual like that involving any other aquatic insect.

Don't worry. No one is going to *make* you eat one of the damn things, although it is regarded as impolite to refuse one when offered.

The Crowds

The setting: Melrose, Montana, during the second weekend in June. Something is obviously happening here in Melrose. Fifty weeks a year, this is a pleasant, fundamentally sleepy little town where folks wear jeans and cowboy boots and talk about rainfall and cattle prices and not a whole lot more. Now it is choked with people and vehicles, every one of which seems to have a MacKenzie riverboat in tow. The dress code for the invasion is eclectic above the waist, but below the belt everyone is clad in waders. The epicenter of activity is the nearby stream access site on the fabled Big Hole River. Trucks and boat trailers jockey for position at the ramp. Despite the apparent chaos, the process of getting boats into the water is going well. The flares of temper that often mar such efforts elsewhere are notably absent, which should tell you something about life in Melrose, Montana.

Study the participants in detail and you will recognize several distinct populations: guides struggling to maintain the appearance of professionalism, half the adult population of Butte, a smattering of refugees from Fortune 500 corporate boardrooms looking uncomfortable with the loss of their customary sense of command. Each group has its own field marks. Guides' clients: chest-high neoprene waders, graphite rods, elegant reels, fishing vests, wooden nets. Locals: hip waders, aged fiberglass rods, creels, and coolers full of beer. Everyone seems to be having a good time. This point seems worth emphasizing.

Now that you've come all this way, it's time to face a measure of reality. If your composite image of a day on a famous Montana trout stream includes adjectives like *serene* and *uncrowded*, you are in the wrong place. Salmon-flies attract fishermen even more reliably than they attract fish. If company bothers you a lot, there are a few tricks that may allow you to enjoy The Hatch with some measure of calm. You can wake up at four in the morning and get several hours downstream ahead of the crowds. You can ignore the dry-fly fishing completely, go miles above the hatch, and fish Bitch Creek nymphs against the bank, in which case you will see relatively few anglers and catch plenty of fish. In the end, however, I find it more productive simply to acknowledge that man is a social animal. Just as New Orleans has Mardi Gras, Kentucky has the Derby, and Pamplona has bulls, Montana has The Hatch. Those in search of a wilderness fishing experience should go to the wilderness. I certainly do my share of that, but this is another matter entirely.

I know. As a first-time participant you expected something more sedate, more solitary, more . . . western. There is plenty of that to be had out here beneath the Big Sky, but not here, not now. My advice? Relax and enjoy the show.

The Rivers

If fishing The Hatch involved floating monotonous water through unattractive surroundings, its critics would certainly have a stronger argument. Fortunately, such is hardly the case.

The salmon-fly enthusiast's travel itinerary reads like a required list of classics. It is no accident that the same waters that support giant stoneflies also support giant trout. I know of no Montana stream with a salmon-fly hatch that is not also a great trout stream in its own right the rest of the year.

Each of the heavyweight waters has a character all its own, and since the bugs' peak emergence occurs at different times on most of them, the ambitious angler with time to spare can turn The Hatch into a smorgasbord of fishing experiences stretching over nearly two months. Begin in late May on Rock Creek with its fast-paced boating and fish-laden pocket water. Move on down to the Big Hole, where the current runs the color of weak tea and pushes its way up into the willows, bringing the five-pound browns right along with it. Check out the lower Yellowstone, and hope you can squeeze in a day or two of fishing before the runoff sends you packing. Then head back overland to the Madison where it will be happening somewhere along the course of that proverbial hundred-mile riffle right on into July. If you haven't burned yourself out by this time, you can return to the upper Yellowstone and chase the last of the flies up into the Park, until you look up one day and realize that it is the middle of the summer and time to get on with the rest of your life.

Of course there are other streams with salmon-fly hatches. Some have fewer flies, some have fewer fish, and most have fewer people. Certainly some anglers might find comfort in their relative quiet. But the Blue Ribbon streams are the classics, and tradition is very much a part of the salmon-fly mystique. Each year when June rolls around, there are days when I want to be on the Big Hole and nowhere else in the world, no matter what. And that is right where you'll find me.

The Fish

Finally.

I am standing with my knees braced against the boat's forward deck. My friend Dick LeBlond is at the oars. Dick is plenty good at this. Fishing The Hatch from a driftboat is a two-man team event, and we have had a lot of practice together. Dick is keeping the driftboat checked just so against the current. Our speed is constant, with the right amount of relative velocity between the boat and the river to allow the fly a perfect float every time it hits the water. Our position never varies in relation to the long, willow-lined bank, so the length of my line remains constant from cast to cast. It is early. Nothing has happened, nothing is happening. Still, our eyes remain fixed to the grotesque clump of hook and hair floating along beside us thirty feet away. It is not a Sofa Pillow or a Baird's Stone Fly, but my very own version of the theme: an elk-hair, orange-poly, brown-hackle monster churned out from my tying bench in the middle of the winter when it was twenty below zero outside and I had nothing better to do than think about salmon-flies.

Lift, false cast once, lay out the same familiar length of line, drift. Fishing The Hatch quickly acquires a cadence all its own. We have been at this for an hour. First I rowed and Dick fished, then we traded places. If I hook a fish, we will trade places again, according to house rules. The rower has no reason to feel left out. His job is every bit as critical as the angler's, and the fly is so easily visible that he can follow its course along the current and appreciate the take when it comes every bit as easily as the party holding the rod.

There was no reason to be out here so early this morning except that we wanted to be. Now the sun is warming the water at last. Bugs are starting to crawl about on the willows, surreal in size and outline. Spotting the first naturals of the day lends sudden validity to what has been largely an abstract exercise. Dick checks the boat a bit more intently. I roll the bulky fly even more perilously close to the willows. And then it finally happens.

Given the bugs' size and the degree of anticipation here in the boat, one would expect something of a production when the take occurs, something akin, say, to a bass smacking a surface plug or a tarpon inhaling some gaudy streamer. Not so. One minute the elk-hair fly is bobbing along in the current like a child's bathtub toy and the next minute it is simply gone. We both stare for an instant at its absence, until Dick yells something inarticulate and I strike back. Then the rod kicks, the reel screams, et cetera, just the way it is supposed to happen in all these stories. The fish on the end of the line looks like a brown. With the current behind it, the trout leads us through fifty yards of good water before Dick can check us into an open spot on the bank. Minutes later, the trout rests quietly in the net.

One of the often-repeated tales of my childhood misdeeds concerns the November day when my father and I returned from a long grouse hunt to a well-deserved Thanksgiving dinner. Cold and tired, I put our bird dog on the back porch instead of kenneling him. Unbeknownst to me, my mother had removed the Thanksgiving turkey fresh from the oven to the same back porch. If you can imagine what a sixty-pound short-hair looks like after consuming an entire twenty-five-pound turkey, you can also imagine the appearance of a typical brown trout during the peak of the salmon-fly hatch. This one looks gravid. The golden sides are taut and distended, the red spots seemingly stretched near the breaking point. As I bend to slip the hook free, I notice the rear half of a natural protruding from its gullet right next to my imitation. The fly is still wiggling. Evidently, nature does not acknowledge gluttony as one of its deadly sins.

Rods clatter as Dick and I trade places. I set my shoulders into the oars in order to pull us out of the willows before we break something. In the bow, Dick is already establishing his own version of The Hatch's rhythm. After several stanzas of lift, cast, and drift, his own hair-and-feather version of *P. californica* disappears. I maneuver us into a backwater where Dick eventually nets the fish. As we trade places again, the current catches our stern and sweeps us in a wild pirouette. Willows slap at our faces and threaten our rod tips with disaster. Before we finish our trip past this long straightaway, we will have hooked five trout, landed three, and remembered beyond a doubt why we came here.

The typical Fabulous Salmon-Fly Hatch story will go on to imply a whole day of this sort of thing, with participants catching huge trout until they can no longer stand it. Alas, reality intrudes. The flurry of activity subsides as it usually does, leaving us to work our way on down the river to the creak of the oarlocks and the hypnotic rhythm of lift, cast, and drift. A whitefish rises, intent on getting the #2 dry fly into its #12 mouth, to no avail. The sun bears down harder. I catch another brown, Dick picks up the day's first rainbow. Long-billed curlews chastise us from a nearby nesting area. I stop, take pictures, go to sleep in the sun. Late in the morning there is another flurry. We hit six quick fish and then the river turns quiet, and we stop again for lunch.

This is how it really goes during The Hatch. If you arrive thinking that being on the best of all possible rivers at the best of all possible times guarantees fifty-fish days with more five-pound trout than you have ever seen in your life, you will usually be disappointed. So don't. Come here instead because it is fun, which it certainly is.

And fun is never disappointing.

There you have it, the mystique of the salmon-fly hatch deconstructed at last. It *is* fun watching gluttonous trout rise to inhale flies that look like baby dinosaurs, and it is important to defend that sense of childish pleasure. Much of the fly-fishing revival of the last two decades seems to have lost track of this basic fact. Perhaps it's just that I am a blue-collar,

Muddler-Minnow kind of guy at heart. I am forty-six years old now, and can document that I have been fishing with flies for more than forty of those years, and can remember quite well enjoying the process even before I knew the names of the insects I was trying to imitate with homemade flies that didn't really imitate much of anything, at least by contemporary standards. I felt no real need to master the stream or acquire an academic knowledge of insect life or be better at catching fish than anyone else. I did it because it was fun. And I still do. Because it still is.

The fact is that The Hatch takes us back to our roots. And that is finally the important lesson for those familiar with the fly fisher's craft but acquainted with giant stoneflies only by hearsay. The Hatch may be congested, frustrating, and unreliable. It is seldom all that you have previously heard it made out to be. But it is fun, crowds and bugs and all, and that promise always seems enough to get me back again next year.

Perhaps it will be enough to get you there someday as well.

Chapter 11

Huck Finn Lives

 *The hills and river cliffs we passed today exhibit a most romantic appearance. The bluffs of the river rise to a height of from two to three hundred feet, and in most places perpendicular. They are formed of remarkable white sandstone . . . .*
—Meriwether Lewis; May 31, 1805

It has been a long, dusty drive north from town across the prairie and into the breaks. Shadows lengthen as we pull the three pickups into the undeveloped camping area where we will spend the night. This is the magical hour when golden colors spread across the dry plains and mule deer begin to appear from nowhere, feeding their way delicately out of the coulees toward the open ground. The three-note woodwind dirge of mourning doves rises from the cottonwoods along the river as the summer heat finally begins to loosen its grip on the arid land. There is no one here other than ourselves.

The Missouri looks utterly imposing as it crawls along in front of camp like a great bloated snake. The current moves at an even crawl, its surface free of all disturbance. The river is wide enough here to accommodate a float plane landing sideways, perpendicular to the axis of its flow. Even in the tricky light, you can see that the water runs brown and plain as dirt.

It doesn't look like a trout stream and it isn't. *That* Missouri (the one with the stately guide boats and the five-pound browns, the one you probably expected to read about in this book) lies a hundred miles upstream, which is a good place for it as far as I'm concerned. It took dams to make that Missouri a trout stream, and if you hate dams on free rivers as much as I do, it seems hypocritical to enjoy fishing their tailwaters.

There will be no trout on this trip. We will be floating the White Cliffs section of the Wild and Scenic Missouri, a long corridor of natural wonders whose eerie beauty moved its first explorers to lyrical descriptions nearly two centuries ago. And while we have chosen this section for its grandeur and its solitude, there will be fish, although they may not necessarily be the kind of fish you expected, and we will catch some, although not necessarily by Queensbury Rules. Let's hope no one has a problem with that.

Right now what I know is that I am hot and dry and thirsty and that I am not alone in my opinion. Chaos rules as we haul gear from the trucks and assign chores to the kids. There seems to be a dozen of them, although it is only Nick, Brooke, Nicole, Scott, and Clea, their various siblings having begged off to ride horses, play soccer, or whatever. Soon they have the tents erected, at which point they desert the work force to go look for frogs.

Ray has the ice chest out, and by the time the kids are gone he's got six cold ones lined up on a convenient log. As it turns out, he's not the only one who thought this country deserved a drink:

At 12 o'clock, we came to for refreshment and gave the men a dram, which they received with much cheerfulness—and well deserved.
                    —Meriwether Lewis; May 31, 1805

Nick and Brooke are in one canoe while Joe and Karen occupy the other. Ray and Janice and Clea are in the Stalmaster raft while Lori, Scott, Nicole, and I bring up the rear in my trusty Avon, the veteran of more miles of wilderness river travel than I care to remember. All four craft will have to find their own pace out there, but I know that no one will get too far ahead of us because we've got the beer.

The morning breaks cool and clean as all get-out, and we're on the water early to enjoy the most pleasant hours of the day. The kids are still grumpy with sleep, but Scott wants to fish, and that kind of impulse always deserves attention. Soon Lori and I have got him all rigged up and he's fishing, bringing great happiness aboard the boat to everyone but Nicole who, like ten-year-old big sisters everywhere, cannot abide the thought of her younger brother having a good time, especially at six o'clock in the morning.

We are fishing for walleyes. I know that this is a fly-fishing book, but in this chapter we're all just going to have to take a break. I know, I know. We're all purists here at heart, but I still subscribe to the sixties view that it is possible to adhere to the moral high ground and have fun too. If I thought there was any chance of coaxing a walleye dinner from this river with fly tackle, I would be trying my best to do so.

But there comes a time when you do what you gotta do, and I can't think of a fish that deserves the honor of this seduction more than the walleye. Fly fishers certainly have no more worthy counterparts than Serious Walleye Fishermen, who take their passion to heights every bit as ludicrous as we take our own. We dither over hatches and tippets, they dither over bottom structure and the barometer, and I cannot help but think that the dithering is all pretty much the same in the end.

With a life full of fly rods, longbows, and shotguns, I don't have time to be a real SWF myself, but I have friends who do. Listening to them talk about walleyes is like listening to aficionados talk about the green drake hatch on Henry's Fork. I mean, they do go on. Listening to an earnest discussion between SWFs is a good way to get a feel for what our own clubhouse discussions must sound like to the uninitiated. One thing's for damn sure, I never really know what they're talking about.

But here we are, drifting down the Missouri at first light, watching the sun come up over the same white cliffs that Meriwether Lewis once described so poetically. I'm at the oars with a coffee cup balanced between my knees, Lori is studying the bird book, Nicole is looking for trouble, and Scott, God love him, is fishing. All I ask of the river today is a smooth ride downstream and a walleye dinner, in anticipation of which I have laboriously packed everything needed to prepare it.

Without a single SWF in our party, it's hard to know just how to approach the problem of coaxing fish from the river. Debriefing friends in the know has given us some ideas, but we're still basically boneheads when it comes to walleyes. For now, the best I can do is subscribe to the Infinite Number of Monkeys theory, which implies that having lines in the water is the important thing, no matter what happens once they get there.

Leave it to kids. Before I'm halfway through my high-priority cup of coffee, Scott has started squealing and his rod tip makes it obvious that he's hooked something other than the bottom of the river. Like all good eight-year-olds, he responds to the strike by trying to reel the fish right up through the guides, and it's all over before I can stop him. "Damn," I mutter, thinking of the lost contribution to our hypothetical walleye dinner.

"Shoot," Scott says, thinking of whatever kids his age think of when they have just lost a fish they badly wanted to catch. His near success has aroused the rest of us, and ten minutes later we're all fishing. Having been coached prior to our departure by SWF friends, the technique is vertical jigging.

True SWFs approach vertical jigging with reverence, and regard other walleye methods the way the snootiest dry-fly enthusiast might regard single-egg patterns or Bitch Creek nymphs. Nonetheless, it's hard for me to get over its obvious resemblance to what used to be known as self-abuse: mindless, repetitive, up-and-down motions sustained by the conviction that gratification will eventually result if you keep at it long enough. Oh well. You do it your way, I'll do it mine.

The river is carrying us along easily into a Charlie Russell panorama of sculpted sandstone. Sun warms the rafts as we drift along in tandem, and the current requires nothing but an occasional pull on the oars to keep us going just the way we want to go. The living is so perfectly easy that I'm nearly asleep at the helm. It's almost painful to imagine Lewis and Clark laboring upstream through this same stretch of river with their heavily loaded vessels:

> . . . the men are compelled to be in the water even to their armpits. . . . Added to this, the banks and bluffs along which they are obliged to pass are so slippery, and the mud so tenacious, that they are unable to wear their moccasins . . . . In short, their labor is incredibly painful and great, but those faithful fellows bear it without a murmur.
>
> —Meriwether Lewis; May 31, 1805

No vertical jigging for those guys. I've always been an advocate of going with the flow myself.

Suddenly Ray is whooping in the raft beside us. Whatever he's jigged up from the brown prairie current is strong and powerful, but it is the absolute sense of surprise that is really causing all the excitement. It just does not seem possible to have made contact with anything down in the murk, much less something that actually might be good to eat. Then he's got the fish up to the surface next to the raft. It is indeed a walleye of five or six pounds, a damn handsome fish in its own way, and when it comes over the side there is a feeling of satisfaction about the catch ordinarily reserved for glamour species like steelhead or permit. There is a lesson here, about assumptions and the pleasures of new experiences. Being a Serious Fly Fisher should never degenerate into an excuse for being a snot.

It is late afternoon. The white cliffs have turned into a sort of solar oven, reflecting the sun's rays back and forth across the water until the heat becomes all but unbearable. I have been out in the water in my swimming suit for the last several miles, rolling about on the surface like a seal as I follow the rafts and the canoes downriver. Hot as it is out here, I glide along content in the knowledge that I may well be the most comfortable person in central Montana.

Finally I kick my way to the Avon and heave myself over the side. The kids are getting cranky after a long day of confinement. They don't want to swim. They don't want to fish. Lori, whose kid instincts are second to none, finally suggests that Nicole visit Clea in the Stalmaster raft, and that proposal is just exciting enough to make everybody happy. With his sister out of his hair, Scott wants to fish again, and soon all three of us are vertical jigging as if this fundamentally brain-dead activity were the most rewarding pastime imaginable.

Shadows have finally started to crawl across the river, suggesting that it may be time for dormant fish to awaken. Sure enough, within a matter of minutes Lori has a fish on. Her catch turns out to be a two-pound sauger. SWFs like to turn up their noses slightly at the mention of sauger, an odd attitude toward a fish that most people have trouble distinguishing from walleyes in the first place. No one is putting on airs in this boat though, not when dinner is looking like one walleye divided eleven ways.

I'm busy looking for landmarks. I want to camp where Lewis and Clark did, just for the hell of it and the sense of history, and their May 30 camp upstream from Pablo Island would be just the place. My mind is full of the mental clutter that comes from trying to match the topo map to the terrain around us when something soft and heavy asserts itself against the rod tip, and it takes a moment to realize that this event is the objective of an entire day's worth of vertical jigging.

The fish feels large and powerful as it bores its way back down into the brown water, and it occurs to everyone aboard that this is one we would very much like to land. I slip and fall amidst the inevitable clutter that accumulates after a long day in a raft full of kids. Lori is doing her best to keep my end of the boat pointed toward the fish. Scott is making a tremendous amount of noise. I can't help but note just how much fun everyone is having.

Finally the fish is at the surface where, because no one has thought to bring a net, I must reach out precariously and snag its gill plate by hand. It is another good-sized walleye, virtually identical to the fish Ray took earlier. Dinner is secure, our day complete. We drift around one last bend and there is Pablo Island, staring us right in the face. When we pull in to the left bank and secure our camp right where Lewis and Clark did 189 years, one month, and sixteen days earlier, it feels just like coming home.

Catching fish, releasing fish, killing fish—it's a difficult subject, but one that I think benefits from reflection, not the rigid application of dogma. The fact that releasing sport-caught gamefish is often in everyone's best interest has somehow given rise in certain circles to the confused notion that releasing fish is always morally mandatory. This idea bothers me, not because I entertain fantasies of stuffing my freezer with fish, but because it smacks of political correctness and the triumph of emotionalism over biology that threatens to ruin so much of what is wonderful about outdoor sport.

Release fish? You bet. If it's a wild steelhead or a native cutthroat, you gotta. If it's a Blue Ribbon rainbow or spring creek brown, you oughta. But then there are a whole lot of circumstances where the choice should be pretty much up to you.

One thing I do feel strongly about, though, is that if you do kill a fish, you should honor it properly on the table. Nothing is more insulting to the resource than a dumptruck full of freezer-burned salmon. The decision to kill a fish should never be made casually. It should be made for a specific reason, and the best reason I know is to serve it fresh to an appreciative audience of family and friends.

So here we are. The first trick is to get the fish filleted properly without getting the meat full of sand and other distractions, a task performed in this case on the blade of an oar. Because weight was not a consideration in our packing, I have the luxury of a big cast-iron skillet, a wonderful asset when it comes to dispersing heat evenly from the small burner on the Coleman stove. We have everything laid out carefully in sequence on a downed cottonwood log: seasoned flour, beaten egg with a dash of soy sauce, breading. The fillets pass through this assembly line and into the skillet's perfect sizzle, and in a matter of minutes it's time to eat.

The kids line up first as the initial batch of fried fillets clears the stove. I reach across to one of the plates and break off a sample, just to be sure we're doing everything right. As that bite disappears inside my mouth, I suddenly realize one reason why SWFs get to be the way they are. Walleye enjoys a cultish reputation on the table that happens to be absolutely deserved. Tonight, it's so good it almost brings tears to my eyes.

The kids eat hungrily, but with no real appreciation. The walleye fillets could be cafeteria fish sticks as far as they're concerned. The adults know better, even Karen, who is not a real fish enthusiast. The second batch disappears to a chorus of true enthusiasm. There is more, and we will polish off every last bit of it. Ray raises his beer glass toward the gently darkening sky. "To the walleyes," he suggests, and we all return the toast.

Who knows? Perhaps a SWF will be born tonight.

The sky is cool and calm as I set off along the bank, sliding along in the same slick mud that bedeviled Lewis's men in 1805. The moon has not yet risen, but there is enough light left in the summer sky to let me see where I am going and do what I want to do. What I want to do is to catch a fish from this awkward river on a fly.

A little creek winds down through the cliffs and joins the river half a mile above our tents. As we floated into camp, I noticed an accommodating stretch of water at its mouth, with a broad sandbar alongside that should allow me to cast unobstructed in the dark. Overhead, nighthawks whistle through the air, generating an odd chorus of beeps in the progress of their evening hunt. I blunder right into a mule deer browsing in the willows that line the bank, and the percussion of its hooves echoes through the night as it retreats uphill into the cliffs. The river is so peaceful, and I am so content.

I've got my six-weight rod rigged with a weighted Clouser Minnow, which seems like a perfectly reasonable way to begin. Cool water licks its way up my bare calves as I wade out into the river and begin to cast. What lies beyond is unknown, and that mystery is part of the immense pleasure.

A dozen casts later, damned if I don't actually hook a fish. It seems too much to hope that it might be a walleye, and it isn't, but that no longer matters now that dinner is out of the way. Cornered in the shallows after a brief, silent fight, my prize gives up easily and comes to rest in my outstretched hand. It is a goldeye, and its silver flanks glow luminously in the last light from the western sky. I'll settle for this. I've done what I came to do.

The kids are all conked out beneath the stars by the time I arrive back in camp. Lori and I sit down on the cottonwood log that served earlier as our kitchen table and listen to the river passing by in the night. Neither of us speaks. There is nothing that needs to be said.

This morning, we set out at an early hour and proceeded as usual . . . passed a handsome river which discharged itself on the larboard side. . . . The water of this river is clearer, much, than any we have met. . . . Captain Clark, who ascended this river much higher than I did, thought it proper to call it Judith's River.

—Meriwether Lewis; May 29, 1805

We are nearing the end. The white cliffs are behind us now and we have spilled out into a broad riparian plain studded with rolling hills. Swallows work eagerly across the surface of the water. Vast schools of carp line the banks, finning gently in the sun with their huge golden scales displayed like plates of armor.

A broad expanse of cottonwoods appears on the right bank, where the Judith enters. Clark, the incurable romantic, named this delicate little stream for his girlfriend, whom he later married. Of course, her name was actually Julia. Leave it to Clark to get his own fiancée's name wrong.

It's all denouement now as we drift the last few miles downstream to our takeout. We have some fifty river miles behind us and we have not seen another soul. The sound of a vehicle's tires on gravel rises from the county road to the south. We have returned, although to what is not quite clear.

I feel older and wiser somehow here at the end of the river's tutelage. It has reminded me of these things: that the pleasures of fishing are not enhanced by confining notions of propriety; that passing along unfettered waters is as important to our sense of cultural identity now as it was to our predecessors two centuries earlier.

These lessons are enough for one weekend.

Chapter 12

A Creek for All Seasons

Spring

"April is the cruelest month . . ." At least that was Eliot's view; perhaps he had tax problems. You can bet he never shivered his way through a high-plains winter, with snow wrapping the country in loneliness and wind slicing through his clothes like a knife. Times like that create a respect for spring that yields to no metaphor. Out here, April is when you start to feel like a survivor.

At first it's a matter of day-night cycles, something that starts deep in the pineal gland and spreads slowly to the articulate part of the brain. Then distinct external cues begin to drive the sense of awakening: a raccoon's track in the snow, long Vs of northbound geese undulating against the sky, the liquid sound of ice melting from the roof and falling outside the window as I write. Flush with the realization that one of my five cardinal senses has lain dormant for months, I wander aimlessly through the woods just to enjoy the pleasure of smelling them again.

Then I realize that I am searching for some missing ingredient, like a chef fretting over an unsatisfactory sauce in the kitchen. I shoot my bow, work the dogs, and practice with the turkey call, all to no avail. The final measure of satisfaction remains elusive. Finally the recognition strikes like an epiphany: It's time to go fishing again.

The process seems awkward at first, like kissing an old girlfriend you haven't seen in years. I have to hunt around for the reel, oil it, attach it clumsily to the rod butt. The leader must be replaced and the knots feel foreign and unfamiliar. The fly boxes are a mess, with everything from midges to Muddlers piled together in soft, undisciplined heaps. In another month I'll be able to reach out blindly, like a surgeon in an operating room, and put my hand on whatever I need to catch fish, but now my efficiency rating is zero, and it takes half the morning just to get started. Not that I've got anything better to do.

Down at the creek, the water is just starting to feel the first of the lowland runoff. The upper creek is the place to be. It never muddies up badly, and even with the strong swell of spring in its current the water here looks like one long invitation to a fly line.

The banks are piled high with corn snow. Green shoots edge forth along its margins like the stubble of a day-old beard. The willows gleam brown and bare in the sun, a forest of switches waiting for the infraction of some imaginary rule. The snow crunches loudly beneath my waders. Turned rotten by the sun, it will not support my weight, and soon I am floundering in its grasp like a doomed moose waiting for the wolves.

After twenty yards of desperate aerobics, I finally reach the creek and slide in, savoring the ease of my return after the long season of absence. Eyes closed gently, I listen to the familiar music of the water as it presses around the sudden obstruction of my boots and goes on along its way. It does not seem possible that another year has passed, that the creek has waited all this time to begin all over again without holding any grudges.

It's too early for blue-winged olives, too early for anything except the process. A Bead-Head Hare's Ear feels appropriate to the occasion, and I dig a #16 out of the chaos inside my nymph box. Again the knot evokes a certain awkwardness, exaggerated by eyes that are yet another year older. Then everything is in place, and it's time for the first cast of the season.

It's not that you forget how over the long winter. You just lose a certain sense of intimacy, with the water, with the rod, with your casting arm. The Bead-Head's extra little molecule of weight is just enough to compromise my rhythm, and the nymph hits the water framed by an amateurish corona of line. The current straightens out the mess as it passes and I wade deeper into the heart of the run, searching for the means to reestablish my familiarity with the water.

Some skills cannot be forgotten, and this is one of them. My feel for the line returns quickly, building with each cast. By the time I've worked my way up into the first riffle, even the awkward tick of the Bead Head against the tightened line is manageable by instinct alone, and fishing the next pool feels as effortless as a slow dance with someone you love.

Only a hopeless optimist would expect fast fishing at this time of year, and I certainly know better. Nevertheless, after half an hour of working the flaws out of my neglected technique, I'm ready for something a little less abstract than batting practice. Then the line hesitates out in the middle of the current. Reflexes atrophied by disuse, I stand and watch the take without reacting. Fortunately, the trout are also slow after the long off-season, and this one stays fast to the hook despite my incompetence.

There is no reason to try to make the fight sound like an epic. The little trout shakes and flashes down in the current for a minute or so, and then it yields easily to fatigue, as if it knows I'm going to release it anyway. A rainbow perhaps twelve inches in length, it looks cold and docile lying on its side with the Bead Head dangling from the corner of its mouth. I ease the hook free and watch the rainbow flick its tail and disappear, content in the knowledge that another season has come 'round at last, and that once again I can count myself among the survivors.

Summer

June is when I really start to feel my age. The long summer evenings stretch on for hours after work, and the fishing is so good that I can't stand not to be there. The result is standup midnight dinners and sleep deprivation, challenges that I just can't handle the way I did a dozen years ago. There are several obvious solutions to the problem, but I have yet to choose one that involves less fishing.

The skies have been generous this year, and the pastureland along the lower creek feels so lush that it's hard to believe ranchers could ever go broke in this country. The alfalfa field behind me looks like a hundred-acre spinach salad. Across the creek, cows are lowing stupidly at nothing, but I can't complain. They will feed somebody someday, and since I live and work in a ranching community, that somebody will ultimately feed me. I don't much care for cow shit in the creek, but it's a real world that we live in, every bloody one of us.

The evening is pleasantly warm in shirtsleeves, but far from sweltering. The field is alive with the sound of crickets. A killdeer skitters away along the bank as I approach the creek, trying to seduce me away from her hidden brood. I play my part, pretending to believe her wing is broken until she takes noisily to the air. A pair of mallards whistles by overhead, returning to the creek from last year's stubble. I feel immensely comfortable with all of this, as comfortable as a British aristocrat settling into a familiar leather chair inside his club.

The air above the water is full of insects: emerging evening duns, stately spinners, frantic caddis hurtling about like lunatics who haven't been taking their medications. Swallows swoop and glide with exquisite precision. A waxwing flutters from the brush, plucks some morsel from the air, and returns to its perch. In the tail of the first pool, fish are rising steadily. The violent industry of all this death and procreation is nearly overwhelming.

There is a time to philosophize and a time to fish, and after a long day full of other people's problems, this evening clearly belongs to the second category. At this time of year, the creek's hatches are so complex that it's often hard to know just what is going on out there even when fish are feeding actively. I watch the tail of the pool for a minute, get my face down near the water to study the life forms sweeping by, and finally decide upon a #18 Pheasant Tail emerger.

The jury seldom deliberates for long before rendering a verdict in cases such as this. As soon as I drop the emerger in front of a feeding fish, a dimple appears upon the tail-out's glassy surface and the creek comes alive. The fish is a chunky rainbow the shape of a football, and it's up and down the pool twice in less time than it takes to tell. The rest of the fish go on about their business, like worried diners at a restaurant trying to ignore a sloppy drunk. Their indifference and the first fish's eager response to the Pheasant Tail are the clues that tell me I can catch every damn one of them if I want.

Well, why not. It's been a long day, a long week, a long life. And it's not as if the creek is going to treat me like royalty every time I visit. The first rainbow comes to rest in a convenient pile of brilliant green weeds; I flick the emerger from its lip, amazed that anything so energetic can be subdued by something so small. The fish disappears at once into the darkening current as I study the water in search of my next triumph.

A fish rises. I cast. Whack. As wonderful as it is standing here in the water with the whole creek at my command, I'm beginning to have my doubts about the ease with which the fish are coming. Can it be that solving problems is more gratifying than enjoying their solution? The second fish conducts itself with honor, but winds up at my feet just as surely as the first. I catch myself studying the water for the next feeding fish even before I've got the fly out of its mouth.

Two more rainbows follow without even the suggestion of a refusal. *Damn, you're good at this,* I swear under my breath. Only later will I realize that this is just the sort of notion that goeth before a fall.

Enough pound-and-a-half rainbows. I hike up the bank and put the crimson sun behind me so I can study the next pool for something bigger. Fish are rising inside the current at the head of the run. Halfway down the bank, a new cottonwood sweeper forms a blank spot in the flow of current where none is supposed to be. That is where I finally see it: a great bulge of water appearing and disappearing at a fraction of the frequency demonstrated by the smaller fish. This is what I have come for, what the summer night has been smiling about all along.

As I approach cautiously to study the geometry of the problem, enough color appears in the rise form to establish that my quarry is a brown. As I watch the fish feed, the final complexity of the situation becomes apparent. The big fish has two pawns stationed just outside its own impregnable lie, and to present a fly to the fish I want, I will have to drop the leader right on top of these cohorts without spooking the whole lot of them. Of course, strategy like this is just what enabled this fish to attain its size in the first place.

I circle downstream and cross the creek as cautiously as if I am stalking a bedded elk. The sight of one exceptional fish can make you twitchy so fast it's scary. In place at last, I mark the position of the brown and its two lieutenants, gauge the current one last time, and cast. The fly hits the sweet lick of water behind the cottonwood with just enough wow in the line to provide a few seconds of drag-free drift before it disappears to a strike.

I know at once that I haven't done it, and I haven't. It is one of the pawns. The fish runs off into the current and jumps, putting its pink sides on display in the last of the sunlight. I have been taken out by the interference. The big brown will not rise again tonight.

When the rainbow comes to hand at last, I must confront my own selfish sense of disappointment. It's a nice fish in its own right, I tell myself. It's part of the game. Then the devil whispers in my ear: *Take this one home and eat it and you'll have one less problem to deal with when you come back tomorrow.* But that wouldn't be fair, would it: not to the rainbow, not to the brown, not to the creek.

I release the fish, rise stiffly, and study the quiet spot behind the downed cottonwood until there is no more light left on the water. Overhead, bats have joined the fray, fluttering by on leathery fingers extended against the dying sun. They are mammals, I remind myself; warm-blooded and nurturing, one another's mothers and fathers and children. The noise of feeding fish rises from the tail-out of the pool, but I am done with them tonight and they are done with me.

By the time I climb back up the bank and start along the edge of the field toward the truck, I am at peace—with the fish I caught and the fish I did not catch; with invertebrates and vertebrates, cold-blooded and warm; with the day and the days left to come. Where would I be without the creek, I wonder as I stride easily along through the darkness. Tell me: Where would I be?

Autumn

Montana's flora is generally dominated by conifers in the mountains and sage and prairie grasses on the plains. Deciduous trees can be few and far between. My own part of the state enjoys more than its share, and no circumstances promote their enjoyment more than autumn along the creek.

The phenomenon sneaks right up on you at first, since September days are usually warm if not downright hot, scarcely the kind of weather to mark the passage of seasons. Nights are another matter, and by the time I'm getting up in the dark to hunt elk with the bow there is usually a real nip in the air even if it doesn't survive much past dawn. Then one day the foliage along the creek bottoms is streaked with yellow, and before you know it whole valleys are pulsating with more colors than anyone would have imagined possible a few weeks earlier.

The creek is never more beautiful than in the fall, but that is when I neglect it the most callously. The problem certainly has nothing to do with the fish the creek has to offer then, since autumn provides, in addition to spectacular scenery, some of the best fishing of the year. It's just that there are so many other things to do: elk and antelope and grouse, bows and shotguns and retrievers. Thirty days hath September.

If it were up to me it would have about two hundred, and I'd still be pressed for time.

And so I approach the creek today like a straying husband returning home with a guilty conscience. I haven't fished for days. I've driven across the wooden bridge between my house and the county road and looked down into the clear water and seen the fish and the insects, and then I've kept right on driving. Bugling bulls do that to you, I rationalize as I stop beside the creek below town, and I wonder if the creek can forgive my neglect.

It's a five-minute walk to the first feeding lie. The water there tumbles along like liquid crystal, and I can remember drinking vodka that didn't look as clear. From the bank high above the water I can see dark shapes holding midway between the surface and the gravel bottom, and every few seconds one of them sprints across the current to slash eagerly at a nymph. I tie a Hare's Ear to the tippet and drop it just above the nearest fish, and it's feeding time at the zoo.

The fish is a brown, and its determined run upstream quiets the rest of the pool immediately. There is no hurry this morning, and when the trout comes to rest in the shallows I kneel at the waterline to study it. Browns always seem more beautiful in September, as if some of the golden glow of the foliage along the creek has taken up residence in their flanks. The black spots look darker and the red ones more crimson as the fish prepare to move upstream to spawn. When I remove the nymph from the corner of this one's mouth, direct the fish back into the current, and watch it disappear, it seems too beautiful for mere memory to accommodate. Some medium should be up to the task of recording moments like this, but I have yet to discover it.

I collect myself and walk upstream past the quiet water toward the next pool. Across the creek a spotted sandpiper teeters along the gravel like a child's windup toy. A pair of teal flushes from a nearby backwater, and it's hard to imagine that their final departure of the season is only a week or two away. A bull snake glides past my foot in the grass, scaring the hell out of me in the process. It's easy enough to tell yourself that it's only a bull snake, and it's another matter to watch that cold coil of muscle ease by so close to your leg that it makes your skin tingle. My revulsion is a lot of anthropomorphic bullshit, of course; the snake's intentions are no more malign than the sandpiper's. It would be interesting to know what the trout think about us when they see our outlines appear above the nearest bank.

A few smaller rainbows are nymphing in the tail of the pool, but I walk right by them in favor of the run upstream. I don't feel like stalking quarries whose rewards and limitations are clear at the outset. The fast water breaks cleanly over a little riffle and gathers itself against the opposite bank, allowing its turbulence to hide its secrets. If fish are holding there, I'm going to have to find them with the Hare's Ear.

Sight-casting requires you to witness your failures, an indignity spared those fishing blind. Perhaps that's one reason why casting to the current is more relaxing than casting to the fish. Halfway through the run, the leader hesitates and I lift the rod tip right into a trout. It's no bigger than any of those feeding downstream, but it's more impressive somehow, as if magnified by its own unannounced appearance. The creek presents my catch without comment, I offer it right back again, and even the trout seems at ease with the whole process. As Ezra Pound once said of Walt Whitman: Let there be commerce between us.

The next half a mile of water will produce half a dozen more fish. The pace of their taking stays casual and dreamy, with strikes coming just often enough to meet my modest expectations, but never so fast that I must bear down or risk missing something out of the ordinary. The measured rate at which the fish appear allows plenty of time to relax and let the intensity of the hunting season loosen its grip, to forget about the direction of the wind and the noise of boots on gravel and surrender to the spell of fall.

By the time I finally climb from the water and start back along the edge of the field toward the truck, I know that creeks can forgive after all.

If only people could do so well.

Winter

Some kinds of fishing practically invite bitter weather. Steelhead provide one obvious example. It just doesn't feel like you're fishing for them unless wind and rain are involved. I've fished late-season silvers when the air was so cold that you had to thaw out the guides every second or third cast, and I've caught Dollies right out from under slush-ice threatening to seal up the water for the year even with me standing in it.

So I guess there is no intrinsic reason why we should end our relationship with trout streams when the snow flies and the thermometer plummets, especially with spring creeks, where the water temperature scarcely varies and the current stays open all year. A truly hard core angler could do it, with woolens head to toe and fingerless gloves and the heart of a lion. I think about it every winter, and then a wise inner voice asks the obvious question: Are you out of your goddamned *mind?*

Evidently not, at least when it comes to subzero trout fishing, which is just not something I need to do badly enough to make me want to do it. Fishing the creek is an elective exercise, and I do plenty of it under pleasant conditions no matter what the fish are doing. In a way, I hate to compromise this easy relationship by fishing under difficult circumstances that might make me ask more of the creek than I have a right to ask.

That's why I came today, not with rod and reel, but with Sonny and my double and a bagful of decoys. The mallards arrived in sets of eight and ten—plump, perfect birds that filled the frigid air with the sound of their wings as they settled into the blocks. The actual shooting was kid stuff, but Sonny was so happy to see the birds fall that I felt like celebrating each time he hit the water.

Now I am trudging along the familiar bank with the decoys slung over my shoulder and the weight of the mallards pulling against the back of my game vest. The sun is just clearing the mountains to the east, and the ice crystals in the foliage along the creek are brilliant enough to make me squint. The dog is just full of piss and vinegar, romping through the snow in a heedless display of high spirits impossible to ignore. The water vapor condensed on his muzzle gives him the look of a clown, and when he presents himself for my approval I laugh and scratch his ears and watch him dive headlong into the powder all over again.

It is nearly Christmas. I pause on top of the bank and look down at the creek flowing smoothly and evenly despite the bitter cold. Ice just cannot find a purchase there, and it is reassuring to see the creek laugh right in the face of another heartless Montana winter. We should all be able to do the same, I tell myself. If only it were that easy.

I find it difficult even to imagine trout there now, suspended like the subjects of some cruel experiment beneath the cold black surface of the creek. Yet this is the same stretch of water where I caught the first fish of the year back in April, back in the beginning. And they are still there now, doing whatever trout do when the air temperature is five below zero and naked flesh freezes on contact with the wind. Winter is obviously not bothering them all that much, and there's really no reason why it should bother me.

It falls to the creek today to remind me that the whole idea of beginnings and ends is an illusion, one of those lazy mental shortcuts indulged by the human mind to save us from the vertigo of the Big Picture: the infinite endlessness of everything, from mayflies to galaxies.

I pause and stand transfixed, staring at the creek while the dog stares at me. Finally a hint of breeze freshens from the west and it is more than I can endure. I turn my back to the wind and call to the dog and we continue on our way. For the moment, at least, both of us are ready—for winter, for spring, for whatever might come next.

Part III

BEYOND

Finally, after all these pages, an admission: I have always wanted to be a travel writer. It's hard to say just what is so appealing about that strange, quirky genre, but when I read good contemporary practitioners of the art—Bruce Chatwin, say, or Paul Theroux—I often wind up saying to myself, *Yeah, that's the kind of writing I'd like to be doing*. Nonfiction generally doesn't affect me that way, even when it is the work of people admired for their prose.

The appeal of reading and writing about other places has to do with expanding one's own horizons, I suppose, with slipping the surly bonds of culture and seeing the world as some of the rest of us see it. I have always enjoyed a skeptical view of social assumptions (which has sometimes made my life difficult in smalltown America, where such assumptions are often taken very seriously). People like me find travel reassuring because it reinforces our suspicion that much of what goes on back home is every bit as arbitrary and pretentious as it seems.

While I have managed to travel to every continent except Antarctica, my reasons for going to all those obscure places almost always have something to do with hunting or fishing. In fact, it is difficult for me to see the world from any perspective other than the outdoorsman's, which is either a serious character flaw or a matter of confirmed principle, depending on your point of view. With a few reliable exceptions, this leaves me to deal with one of two predictable editorial responses when I start going on about my travels in print: *Nice, but what's this got to do with fishing?* (in the case of dedicated rod-and-reel publications), or *Sorry, we don't do blood sports* (the usual verdict from magazines that circulate beyond the traditional outdoor market).

While there isn't much to say to those in the second category, I would like to protest constructively to those in the first. We all have different reasons for spending as much time as we do fly fishing, most of which have little if anything to do with extracting nutrition from the food chain. Distilled down to their essence, most of those motives have to do with the rediscovery of our own sense of wonder at the natural world. As babies, we can experience that wonder by crawling to the other side of the playpen; as kids, the field behind the house will do. As adults, the search for new horizons becomes more challenging, involving, in the fly fisher's case, new species, new water, and new methods, all driven by the realization that the alternative may be a lifetime of six-packs, couches, and televised football.

Nothing speaks to that need for new experience quite like total immersion in an alien ecosystem, especially if surrounded by an unfamiliar culture. And nothing gets the visitor out of the usual tourist loop as reliably as the challenge of outdoor sport, which requires that the observer negotiate directly with the observed. And while the fish and the fishing are important, they cannot to be taken out of context, which is why the nuances of food, language, and architecture are every bit as central to the experience of angling abroad as selecting a fly pattern or landing a fish.

All of which helps explain why I keep going other places to fish even when I am surrounded by the best fishing in the world. Are bonefish and permit and *plateados* really more worthy opponents than Montana rainbows or Alaska salmon? When all is said and done, you can probably flip a coin. If you insist on justifying the time, energy, and expense of travel to exotic destinations on the basis of the fish themselves, there is always a possibility you will be disappointed. Better to fish those places for the same reason Hillary climbed Everest: because they are there.

A growing number of anglers seem to feel the same way about all this, and nothing marks the emergence of the adventure-angling phenomenon quite like the proliferation of rod cases in the airports of the world. Stand at the baggage claim carousel at ANC or BIL at the right time of year and you'll see more fishing gear than suitcases circling that nervous perimeter of waiting passengers. And then there are the guys who haul their four-piece take-downs as carry-on luggage, as if they just can't bear the thought of even a temporary separation. I counted over a dozen of them in the Salt Lake City airport recently, in the middle of winter no less. I always regarded that habit as an affectation, until the airlines lost my bags on a bonefish trip and I spent three days pounding the flats with a borrowed rod. Now I carry mine with me all the time too.

While I have never pretended true expertise with the fly rod, the first two sections of this book were at least written with a certain authority, the kind that constant exposure to a subject affords even to rock-heads like me. Now we're entering new territory. It would be ridiculous for me to assume real understanding of permit or sea-run browns based on occasional visits to their haunts. Don't worry. I have no intention of insulting your intelligence or my own.

What follows instead is a wide-eyed look at some favorite exotic fishing destinations written more from the perspective of Alice in Wonderland than Joe Brooks: seven chapters, seven countries, five languages, a dozen species of fish ranging in reputation from the sublime to the ridiculous. My interest lies in the feel of the places and the people and the water and, sure, the fish. And I'll do my best. But if you want someone to tell you what to do when you get there, you're in the wrong department. You'll have to figure that out for yourself, but that's half the fun.

It's impossible for me to review this section without being struck by two amazing quantities: the number of places I have managed to fish and the number of places I haven't. Personally, the second list is even more intriguing than the first. I've never fished for Atlantic salmon, a cultural deprivation that practically qualifies me as a *victim* of some kind. I've never teased up a sailfish or pounded the surf for stripers. There are tiger fish in Zimbabwe, dog-toothed tuna in New Guinea, peacock bass, mahseer, dorado—the list goes on, farther, obviously, than I ever will. And that is the final, wonderful source of satisfaction that derives from the thought of addressing the whole wide world with your fly rod:

No matter how hard you crawl, you never get all the way across the playpen.

Chapter 13

Caviar Flies and Keta

My friend Sergei always reminds me of General Douglas MacArthur's proscription against fighting a land war in Asia. A sable trapper by profession, his features have been tempered by a lifetime in the unforgiving Siberian bush. Scars from one of several bear maulings cover his forearms. His face reflects the mixture of European and Asiatic ancestry common to many of the area's residents. Like most inhabitants of the region, he carries a well-worn military surplus carbine with him everywhere he goes, and I know from experience that he shoots it with uncanny accuracy. At some point during every day I spent with Sergei and his friends, one simple realization occured to me, which was that I am glad we never had to fight the Russians, especially on their own ground. Gulf War technology be damned; it would have been a nightmare.

It is late on a sunny August afternoon. Despite the long northern days, the nights have been crisp enough to leave rims of ice in our water jugs and turn the birches yellow. There is an odd familiarity to these suggestions of an early fall that reminds me of the feel of autumn at home, of football and Halloween and burning leaves, culturally defined events whose memory seems strangely out of place here in the Russian Far East. Not everything seems foreign, though. The current flowing past us toward the North Pacific runs cold and clear and looks as inviting as any stream in Montana. Nothing makes an angler feel at home quite like good water.

Standing next to each other on a long, sweeping gravel bar, Sergei and I prepare ourselves for the task at hand. We have walked down to the river with a mission, which is to produce some dinner for the hungry party back in camp. For the last several days we have lived off a caribou hindquarter, but that is almost gone now and there is nothing much in the pot next to the campfire but onions. After a long day of hiking the tundra with our bows in search of grizzly bears, we have developed the kind of appetites that won't yield to onion soup.

As anxious as I am to start fishing, it is impossible not to study Sergei's own streamside preparations. While I am carrying nothing but my skeleton wilderness fishing gear, I still have a rod and reel and basic accessories. Sergei, on the other hand, is nearly starting from scratch. As I watch, he inspects a pile of fallen timber left behind by the last spring flood, and finally cuts a ten-foot length of tamarac from the tangle. After a few minutes' work with his hunting knife, the dead sapling is a primitive but serviceable fishing rod. From the backpack that contains everything he needs to survive all summer in the bush, he removes a length of stout line and a precious fishhook. Next, he whittles a float from a piece of driftwood and ties everything together. Finally he returns to the backpack and extracts a tin from which he scrapes a few heavily salted fish eggs for the hook. *"Caviar!"* he laughs, and I laugh back, for it is always a happy moment when the two of us can add a new word to our painfully limited common vocabulary.

Meanwhile, I have selected a streamer from my fly book and tied it onto the end of my own leader. There is nothing left to do now but go fishing, and the two of us wade out into the river and begin to address the current and its contents, each in our own way.

The river supports a strong run of *keta*, the familiar Pacific dog salmon. In fact, we have spent the last two days stalking grizzlies along a little spawning stream upriver from our camp where the *keta* are so thick that the water scarcely seems able to accommodate them. Here in the main river, the salmon are fresh from the sea but widely scattered. The Russians have suggested the presence of other species, but the language barrier makes it difficult to imagine what they might be.

There is something hypnotic about the rhythm of fishing a river like this. The steady pulse of the current against my boots seems to insist that all will be well in the end, and after spending several long days getting too close to too many grizzlies, I am ready for just this sort of reassurance.

With the warm Indian summer sun on my back and miles of unspoiled wilderness stretching away from the river in all directions, I find myself yielding to the sort of tranquility you seldom get to enjoy this far north along the wild Pacific rim, unless you're fishing.

Leave it to the fish to interrupt. After a dozen casts, something strikes and retreats immediately to the bottom of the pool to sulk. The fish refuses to jump, and after a brief, dogged fight I ease it up into the shallows; it's a Dolly Varden in the three-pound range. Its flanks are alive with vivid color, and the visual pleasure it provides is almost enough to save it from the pot. But after thinking about the onions and the bedraggled remains of the caribou back in camp, I review my calculations and conclude that the river can easily spare a fish or two, even if they are pretty ones.

Downstream, Sergei is suddenly battling something far more substantial on his own handcrafted tackle. Soon the green-and-maroon flanks of a mature dog salmon appear at the surface in a cloud of spray. It doesn't seem possible that he can land this vigorous fifteen-pound fish with his primitive gear, but he uses every bit of the pole's spring to tease the fish toward shore. When it runs aground at last, he falls on his catch like a hungry bear, and our subsistence fishing anxieties are over.

There is work to be done first. Sergei quickly dispatches the fish, slices through its abdomen with his hunting knife, and removes two brimming skeins of eggs. The tail end of one goes right into the tin of salt, where it will remain like sourdough starter. The remainder of the eggs are sprinkled lightly with salt and rolled into a section of *Pravda* from his backpack. "*Caviar*," Sergei repeats with a grin, and I know that the evening's hors d'oeuvres have been accounted for as surely as the main course.

With dinner for the camp secure, Sergei dismantles his tackle and carefully returns the hook and line to its place in his backpack. Relieved of the obligation to fish like a predator, I wade right back into the stream. I am soon fast to another salmon, whose powerful runs make me wonder how Sergei ever got the job done with his simple complement of sticks and string. Of course, my amazement mirrors the Russians' skepticism about our own ability to handle the grizzlies with our longbows, which only proves that confidence is above all else a measure of belief.

Once the fish is in the shallows, I reach down, back the hook out of its lip, and release it to continue its journey upstream toward destiny.

Sergei poses a question in Russian that I cannot begin to follow. I suspect that he is asking me why I released the fish, an impression that Andrei, the one bilingual member of our party, will confirm later back in camp. I will also learn that none of the Russians have ever seen anyone release an edible fish.

"Fun!" I shout at Sergei, as I point toward the newly liberated salmon retreating toward the main current.

"Fun," he repeats hesitantly.

I hand him the rod, and for the first time since we've met he seems overwhelmed. He takes several steps out into the water and looks back for guidance. I pantomime the motion the rod should make overhead. Several tentative casts later, he is downright getting the hang of it, and within minutes he has hooked a fish, another chunky salmon that makes the reel whine and brings a look of absolute rapture to Sergei's weathered face. It takes a good fifteen minutes to bring this fish to bay. Finally he starts to horse it up onto the gravel bar, but I raise my hand, and when he stops I reach down, twist the hook backward from the fish's jaw, and let it swim away. "Fun," I explain again, and Sergei nods his head slowly in comprehension.

When we finally quit and carry our two kept fish back upstream toward camp, I am all but certain that we have added yet another word to our common vocabulary. It's hard to imagine a more important one.

We spent the next day eating dog salmon soup and trying to get close to bears. Bowhunting grizzlies is one of those undertakings that you just can't do nonstop, for it requires a degree of mental intensity that cannot be sustained indefinitely. The next afternoon, I decided to leave the bow behind and go fishing. Somehow I sensed that I had not yet seen everything the river had to show.

Sergei and I hiked upriver to a long, even riffle that looked as if it could have flowed right out of a western American trout stream—the Yellowstone, perhaps, or the lower Madison. Brooding *keta* sulked in the pool below us and fresh bear tracks surrounded a cluster of picked-over carcasses on the bank. After days of trying to get close to grizzlies I had grown comfortable with their constant presence, but Sergei's carbine still provided a welcome measure of security.

My selection of another bright, generic streamer from the fly book produced a chorus of *nyets* from Sergei. "*Caviar!*" he repeated insistently, and when in a moment of inspiration I produced a single-egg pattern from the fly book, his face erupted in a broad smile. *Caviar. Da.* Somehow, despite the formidable language barrier, we always seemed to get the important things worked out.

I waded into the current and let the egg fly drift down through the riffle. On the third cast, the line hesitated and I struck back. Soon I was admiring a beautiful arctic grayling, with deep purple flanks and an elegant dorsal fin as long as my hand. The amazing thing about the grayling—and the salmon and the Dollies, for that matter—was the way they evoked a sense of familiarity in the middle of the Russian wilderness. The language and the people and the foliage along the riverbanks bore no resemblance to anything I knew. Even the sunsets felt different. But the fish were the same, a common thread woven all the way across the vast Pacific without regard to passports or politics or nuclear warheads, and each time I brought one in toward shore the process felt as reassuring as the arrival of an old friend.

I unhooked the grayling gently, held it up toward Sergei, and coaxed the fish's Russian name from him. The strange word felt awkward in my mouth and made no impression on my memory. I should have been used to this by now—the alien inflections, the utter inability to connect with any of my own linguistic bearings. That was what I found so maddening about Russian: I just didn't get it. "Grayling!" I said to Sergei. "Grayling!" With each syllable, I thrust the fish in his direction for emphasis, but it did no good. He tried, choked on the unfamiliar construction of sounds, and shook his head in despair. In the end we had to accept our own inability to give the fish a name we could share.

I hold grayling in too much romantic esteem to feel good about killing them, even where they abound. We still had an ample supply of salmon back in camp, so I could release the fish without feeling that I had betrayed my companions or their appetites. Once the grayling disappeared, I rose from the water and laughed aloud at the absurdity of it all. Two men representing different cultures travel great distances to a remote river, catch a fish, struggle inconclusively with its name, and return it to the river. You've got to be kidding.

That night vodka appeared around the campfire, along with a salt-encrusted jar of red caviar and a loaf of unleavened bread. Everyone had new stories to tell, of places and bears and fish. The Russians belted their vodka down hard and straight, and made it plain that it would be impolitic of us not to join them. I've pissed off my share of people over the years, but never by refusing to drink with them, and I saw no reason to begin now, not with a potential end to the Cold War at stake.

Andrei Belyev, our interpreter, is a brilliant Muscovite, a cardiac surgeon and whitewater explorer who puns fluently in English and quotes Shakespeare at will. He may have been the ideal communications facilitator or among this wild party of Siberians and Americans, but by the time the cap came off the third bottle of vodka even he was overwhelmed, not least because of heavy involvement in consuming the first two bottles. Finally, the hectic flow of languages short-circuited something in his brain and he gave up, leaving the rest of us to toast the fish and the bears and the company as best we could. Not only did the job get done, but it seemed to become easier as the evening wore on.

Caviar is said to demand an acquired taste; in the case of red caviar, the acquisition may be beyond the reach of anyone born on the New World side of the Pacific. My own discomfort with red caviar has always bothered me, since I pride myself on an adventuresome palate, especially with regard to anything from the sea. It's not a matter of cultural biases against fish eggs either, since I've devoured herring roe on the beaches of Kodiak and slurped down *uni* in sushi bars until my credit cards were ready to explode. But salmon eggs are another matter; goddammit, they look like bait.

But there we were, surrounded by Russians with semiautomatic weapons, and when the lid came off the caviar jar, it was obviously our civic duty to partake. I sliced a heel off the loaf of bread with my hunting knife, covered it with salted eggs, and bit down hard, trying to suppress the memory of sporting goods store shelves lined with jars of salmon roe.

"Not bad," I said to Ray and Doug after a long pause.

"Bullshit," Ray said.

"No, really," I told him.

"I need some more vodka," he protested, as I passed him the loaf and the jar.

"You've had too much already," I said.

"Bullshit," he repeated.

And so it went. Somehow we survived the vodka and the caviar and Andrei's sudden inability to turn one language into another. Together with the Russians we marveled at the stupidity of our respective governments, the complexity of our languages, and the formidable nature of the fish we had caught. We toasted the grizzlies, Yuri Gagarin, and rock 'n' roll. Then we consumed an entire kettle of salmon-and-onion stew and went to sleep.

By the time the sun rose in the east we were all ready to go hunt bears again, for it didn't seem possible that the grizzlies could do worse to us than what we had done to ourselves in a near-lethal outburst of good-will.

The three weeks we spent exploring the Siberian bush that summer passed far too quickly. The morning the helicopter arrived to take us back to civilization (such as it was), we all gathered in camp for an elaborate round of good-byes and an exchange of gifts. I set up my tying vise and turned every bare hook I owned into caviar flies for our Russian friends. I hope they'll keep someone from going hungry someday out in the bush. I also hope they'll help someone have fun.

Wilderness enjoys a remarkable capacity to insulate people from their own affairs. We had been cut off from the world at large throughout our stay, and only after the long flight back to the hub city of Khabarovsk did we begin to appreciate the enormity of the historical transition taking place around us. Our trip had begun during the immediate aftermath of the 1991 August coup. When we passed through Khabarovsk on our way to the bush, tanks still lined the streets. Now the red Hammer and Sickle was gone, replaced by the flag of the Russian Republic. Musicians were tuning their instruments in preparation for a rock concert on the steps of the former Communist Party headquarters. Seventy years of social and political catastrophe was coming undone all around us, and we could only hope that the future would hold something better for our friends.

In our own ways, each of us lost a bit of his heart to Russia that summer. Ray and I were so taken with the place that, when the Russians asked us to come back again in the spring as their guests, we accepted on the spot. The Russians had shown us their country, we had shown them new ways to enjoy it, and in the end none of us could remember how we managed to grow up certain that we were each other's worst enemies.

Ping-Pong opened the door to China. Is it too much to suggest that fish and fly fishing might have been the real catalyst for the Cold War's end?

Chapter 14

Mysteries of the
Sian Ka'an

 Just *getting* there is a mysterious process, especially when you're coming from Montana in the middle of the winter.

As an experienced traveler I've learned to deal with jet lag, but crossing lines of latitude can sometimes be as unsettling as crossing lines of longitude, and nothing emphasizes the capacity of jet travel to disorient quite like the pursuit of bonefish. Yesterday Lori and I stood shivering outside the Billings airport, scarcely able to endure the walk from Long Term Parking to the terminal even in our warmest winter clothing. Today a display of exotic bird life wheels overhead in the vivid tropical sunlight: egrets, ibis, limpkins, and some unfamiliar species that I can't begin to identify. From blizzards to roseate spoonbills; it seems impossible to span these frames of reference in simple numbers of hours or miles.

Finally, Enrique cuts the motor and poles us through one last curtain of mangroves, and the vast Maraville flats open up before us as if we've stepped through a looking glass. Lori and I climb onto the skiff's bow. I work a tan Crazy Charlie and forty feet of fly line into the air with a few quick false casts, and then we settle into the visual discipline of searching for fish. Lori has never seen a bonefish before, and this is a part of my life that I have anticipated sharing with her for months. Of course my expectations are tempered by the quiet fear that she might find everything about this business crazy, including me.

A firsthand demonstration of the art of bonefishing seems in order, so I hold onto the fly rod. When the first school of fish appears, I put the cast too far in front of them, and they change course before reaching the fly. On the second cast I manage to line an overlooked fish and the whole lot explodes in fright, leaving the flat in front of us empty except for the little cumulus clouds of marl that mark their departure. "So that's how you do it?" Lori asks innocently.

"Something like that," I reply, as Enrique offers a sympathetic shrug from the stern.

By the time the second phalanx of bonefish appears, I have worked out some of my inevitable midwinter rustiness. As soon as the fly hits the water the lead fish accelerates and pounces, and when I set the hook with my line hand all the fish race off across the flat as if the devil himself just appeared in their midst. Ten minutes later the fish is resting next to the boat, and Lori and I hop over the side for a better look.

It is a typical Yucatán bone in the three-pound range. Lori turns the fish back and forth in the water, studying the play of sunlight across the sheen of its burnished muzzle. "So this is a bonefish," she muses, as I feel my fears surface. *You've got to be kidding,* I imagine her thinking. *We've come all this way to catch suckers?* But then she looks up and stares me in the eye and announces that she isn't going to rest until she catches one herself.

Lori's fly-fishing apprenticeship on our local spring creek hasn't afforded much experience with the technical demands of long upwind casts. When we spot the next fish, however, Enrique manhandles the skiff into a position that puts at least some of the wind at our backs. Lori's presentation is less than perfect, but I have already been reminded of a simple lesson, that it is a lot easier to tell someone what they're doing wrong than it is to stand in the bow of the boat and do it right yourself.

These bonefish are in a search-and-destroy mood anyway, and as soon as the fly hits the water two of them are arguing over the spoils. When the fish turns to run, Lori whoops and clamps down with her line hand, and that is that. There is nothing left to do but point out that even a three-pound bonefish can snap a tippet on impact if you let it.

The next group of bones gives Lori a chance to do everything right, and she does. This time when the fish turns and runs, she has the fly line running through the guides before she lets herself get too excited. By the end of the fight she is playing the fish like a seasoned veteran, and then it's time to jump over the side of the boat again and admire her first bonefish as Enrique murmurs approval from the stern. "Now I want to catch another one," Lori says, and I know she's hooked as solidly as the fish. How do bonefish cast their spell over anglers so easily?

Let's just accept that as one of life's mysteries.

Stuck out into the Caribbean like a hitchhiker's thumb, the Yucatán Peninsula is a complex amalgam of pre-Columbian history, glittery resort life, and Third World contradictions. While the fun-and-sun ambience of Cancún and Cozumel offers little to the serious outdoor sportsman, those willing to look a little farther down the coast—and off the beaten path—will find a marvelous surprise in store: a world of jungle whitetails, javelinas, ocellated turkeys, and some of the most enjoyable saltwater fly fishing in the world.

In an admirable display of conservationist spirit, the Mexican government acknowledged the unique ecological legacy of the southern Yucatán coast by creating the Sian Ka'an Biosphere Preserve. Lori and I were exploring the area from the Pez Maya Lodge, strategically located near the northern edge of Sian Ka'an, where it offers excellent access to the vast flats of Yu Yum Lagoon and Ascención Bay. A mere five-minute walk along a white-sand beach leads guests to the outlet of Rio Boca Paila, the channel through which the lagoon flows to and from the Caribbean with every tide change. One look at this natural food conduit convinced me that it offers a unique opportunity to take large saltwater species on fly tackle.

The Boca itself fishes best from October to January, when snook, tarpon, and cubera snapper congregate there to feed on outgoing tides. While our early-spring stay wasn't optimal for these species, there are always big barracuda and jacks near the outlet, especially at dawn and dusk. After our first evening meal, we rounded up our heaviest tackle and strolled down the beach to explore the Boca.

The wind and the tide were running in opposite directions, and the channel was a cauldron of activity. As the last orange light drained slowly from the western sky, we could see pelicans and terns working over schools of baitfish just offshore. Then an osprey appeared on the wind currents, towered briefly above the water, and plunged. When it emerged from its own cloud of spray, the fish in its talons was so heavy it could scarcely labor into the air again.

I offered Lori a few last-minute observations on the physics of the double haul and we waded out into the surf. There was something wonderful about the simplicity of casting our big streamers into the gathering darkness, especially after the intensity of our day on the flats. Nothing out there looked delicate or capable of taking offense. Then, as stars began to emerge overhead, I sensed something unusual going on in the sea around us. "Look!" Lori suddenly exclaimed, and I turned to see her kicking the surf into bursts of cool, green light. The channel was alive with phosphorescent organisms ready to discharge at the slightest disturbance. Each time I picked up my fly line a shimmering curtain of light appeared in the night, like some tropical parody of the aurora borealis.

Just as I started to spoil the childish wonder of the moment with a scientific explanation, the tip of my fly rod bucked, a luminous swirl appeared in the current right at my feet, and line began to evaporate from the reel. Before I could say anything, the line went slack again somewhere out in the darkness. I retrieved what was left of the fly; it felt battered by tooth and jaw. Jack? I wondered. Snapper? 'Cuda?

In the end, it remains a mystery, of the sort only the sea can provide.

I've always felt a particular affection for stingrays, despite an appearance that suggests a supermarket tabloid cover story with a title like *Space Aliens Ate My Baby!* I like rays because their presence signifies activity on the flats, and because they seem to enjoy a special association with permit. And as we know, permit fishermen can use all the help they can get.

On the second afternoon, the flat behind the lodge was crawling with rays. I was delighted to see them, for I had planned this trip with two principal sporting objectives in mind. Lori's bonefish had realized the first. Now all I had to do was catch a Yucatán permit on a fly to claim a double-header.

The vast system of flats running from the Boca south to Ascención Bay is certainly one of the most favorable spots anywhere to see lots of permit. Of course, seeing permit and catching permit are two entirely different matters. Believe me, I know.

I had already cast to half a dozen of them, which amounts to a pretty fair afternoon of permit fishing, at least for those who have already come to terms with the species' obstinate attitude toward fly-rod offerings. At this point, Enrique observed quite correctly that the tan McCrab pattern I was using looked considerably darker and plumper than the local naturals. Since I didn't really have a light crab imitation in my fly book, I switched over to a heavily weighted Puff, which had the authority of tradition behind it and seemed just as capable of not catching permit as anything.

We were drifting along easily in five feet of clear water when I saw the disturbance ahead. It was not the delicately stenciled outline of a permit underwater or the haunting flash of a tail waving in the air. In fact, with the afternoon sun in my eyes it was impossible to tell just what was out there, but I knew it was a fish. When I sent the fly whistling toward whatever I had seen, it settled with a plop, and a deep shape swirled behind it and struck. As the fish began to tear across the flat with the fly line hissing through the sea behind it, I dared to imagine I was about to accomplish what I had all but conceded as impossible.

But the fish rather than the fisherman was in charge of this fight; I was little more than an observer. My fingers turned the reel's drag down as tight as it would go, but two-thirds of my backing was gone in less time than it takes to tell about it. Then the line went dead and it was over, my tenuous connection to glory severed as abruptly as it had begun.

"Maybe a permit," Enrique said from the stern. "Maybe a jack. Who knows?"

I didn't, and I still don't. As with the encounter in the Boca the previous evening, the disappointment didn't come from failing to land the fish but from failing to see it, to understand the source of the excitement even though it remained impossible to conquer. No freshwater angling venue can ever tantalize that way, not like the sea. Despite the ache of the uncertainty, it was reassuring to know that whatever it was still swims out there. After all, unsolved mysteries make the best fish stories of all.

By the next afternoon, I had unsuccessfully presented flies to so many permit that I needed a break, from myself and my own expectations as much as from the fish.

Enrique piloted the boat up a long, tortuous channel that eventually emerged from the mangroves into a broad plain covered with palmetto and saw grass. The ecology of the watercourse began to change as we ran. Different fish and plants appeared, and finally, when a blast of spray hit me in the face, I realized that the water had turned as fresh and pure as a trout stream. Enrique explained that we were headed to a freshwater lake, right in the middle of the lagoon. How did it get there? I wondered. How could so much fresh water appear suddenly in the middle of these saline flats? "*Es misterioso*," Enrique replied with a shrug, to which there was no reply.

As the creek opened to reveal the lake, Enrique pulled the boat in against the bank, where a massive structure of hand-hewn stone blocks stood all but overgrown by the encroaching jungle. Lori and I climbed from the boat and approached slowly, trying to imagine what led the structure's ancient architects to build here. Conventional encounters with the remains of vanished cultures are often buffered by the flavor of our own civilization, with the odd mixture of comfort and silliness that implies. Now there was no one here with us except the birds and the jungle, and the ruins' stony silence felt overwhelming.

We know more about the Maya than we were once willing to acknowledge—that they were superb architects, for example, and that they knew far more astronomy and mathematics than their Old World contemporaries, with whom we naturally tend to identify. But there is much that we don't know, too, and the most intriguing question of all may be: What happened to them? How could a civilization so advanced simply disappear? Theories abound, but the essential mystery remains. There are no clues left except these remarkable works of stone, rising from the remote reaches of the Sian Ka'an to remind us how transient our own civilization may someday prove to be.

Lori and I entered the ancient stone temple and sat together in silence trying to imagine why the structure had been built and what might have taken place inside its walls. There were no answers. When we finally walked back out into the sunlight, the ruins' secrets were still intact. At least I had my own difficulties with the permit in perspective.

We were ready to go fishing again, but it felt like time to change gears, to fish for fish as unlike permit as possible. I couldn't imagine a more likely candidate than the barracuda. Voracious as they are, 'cudas pose unique technical problems on fly tackle. They key their strikes to speed translated through distance, which makes them relatively easy game for tube lures and spinning rods. The fly fisher, however, must manage a bulky fly on the end of a lot of line, put the fly through the 'cuda's strike zone without spooking the fish, and strip the fly as fast as theoretically possible.

As we ran back downstream toward the flats, I chopped off the distal half of my permit leader, attached a foot of wire, and tied on a Mylar needlefish imitation. Enrique soon had the skiff positioned sixty feet upwind of a menacing shape that looked less like a gamefish than a saltwater crocodile. My first cast was frankly better than I expected, but the 'cuda ignored the fly. I put the second cast right in front of the fish's nose and stripped for all I was worth. Nothing. After three more near-perfect efforts I was ready to give up and go back to permit, from which even refusals merit a certain degree of honor. As I started to lift the fly from the water, I turned around to see a look of utter bewilderment on Lori's face, and when I turned back toward the front of the boat I saw why: Four feet of barracuda was sailing across the bow at belly-button level—my fly dangling from its jaws, its wicked incisors flashing in the sun.

In fact, its teeth flashed by several inches *below* my navel, which may be why I forgot to set the hook. The surgical procedure this maneuver brought to mind is called bilateral orchiectomy, which isn't something guys like to think about, especially when they're on vacation with their girlfriends. The 'cuda tore off a hundred yards of line at once, and I was so happy to see it going in the opposite direction without taking any of my anatomy with it that I didn't really care when it threw the hook and disappeared. I may have lost this fish, but the species sure gained my attention.

Twenty minutes later we were upwind of another barracuda. The second fish wasn't as hesitant as the first. As soon as the fly touched down it disappeared to a slashing strike, and 'cuda number two was off across the flats. This time there were no concerns about being gelded, and I drove the hook home with authority. My seven-weight rod felt marginal for a fish this size, but it held under the abuse of several torrid runs until the exhausted fish finally lay panting alongside the skiff. Those teeth, I thought. Those muscular, silver flanks; the electrical quality of the barracuda's strike and first run. Why do saltwater fly fishers so consistently ignore offbeat species like barracuda in favor of the predictable comforts of tradition?

Fashion and taste, it seems, offer mysteries every bit as perplexing as the sea.

We spent our last day fishing for bones, which we caught, and permit, which we did not. No surprises there.

At the very end of the afternoon, Enrique poled the skiff up onto yet another flat only to discover that the outgoing tide had abandoned us. As we sat aground at the edge of the channel, he picked up a pair of bonefish tailing sixty yards ahead—the first time we had seen tailing fish all week. With the sunlight behind them, their tails flashed each time they pirouetted above the marl, and we knew that we couldn't leave the flat without trying to catch them.

The footing outside the boat proved soft but manageable. With warm mud oozing up between my toes, I set off eagerly toward the fish, which began to feed their way toward me. When the fly dropped in front of them they both raced toward it, and then the weight of the winner announced itself on the end of the line. All I had to do was hold the rod tip high, try my best to avoid the little mangrove shoots scattered about the flat, and enjoy everything the bonefish had to offer.

As soon as I released the first fish I caught a glimpse of more tails on the other side of the boat, and called for Lori to grab her gear and join me. As we waded across the sand and grass together, the fish began to work their way farther up into the edge of the mangroves. The sunlight was behind us now, and the tails looked like hammered silver as they rose above the waterline.

Lori stalked the fish slowly and methodically, but the impossible geometry of wind and mangrove shoots limited her opportunities to cast. There were three of them, too busy feeding to spook, but every time Lori was about to present the fly they turned and retreated farther into the mangroves, leading her on like sirens. Then the fish swam through one final curtain of brush and disappeared into a shallow jungle so dense we could not follow, much less cast a fly. We could only stare at the empty water and wonder at the improbability of their retreat.

Where in the world were they going back in there? We will let their destination remain the week's final mystery, for it seems appropriate to end on a wistful note rather than with the comfortable objectivity of one more bonefish in hand. Once taken, fish become known quantities, but it is the mysteries that command our attention and demand our return, and it doesn't really matter whether the mystery is as discreet as a permit's stubborn refusal or as sweeping as the disappearance of a civilization.

Chapter 15

Oro y Plata

While literacy is certainly an admirable characteristic, it is possible to be too literate for one's own
good.

I was thinking about Samuel Taylor Coleridge when the first of the
plateados struck. Scholarly evidence suggests that Coleridge derived his
inspiration for *The Rime of the Ancient Mariner* from the records of one
John Davis, captain of the ship *Desire*, who underwent a series of
harrowing adventures during a catastrophic voyage through the Strait
of Magellan in 1593. Now here we were, fly fishing the same venue of
which Coleridge wrote:

> The many men so beautiful!
> And they all dead did lie:
> And a thousand, thousand slimy things
> Lived on and so did I.

Perhaps old Sam simply had another rough night with the opium
pipe, but there was no escaping the fact that Tierra del Fuego inspires a
mixture of awe and apprehension in its observers.

Tom Brady, our host, shares the Scottish enthusiasm for pursuing
sea-run browns at night. The Scots should know; theirs are the only other
Salmo trutta in the world energetic enough to return to the sea. Within

an hour of our late-afternoon arrival at the Estancia San Jose, Tom had fishing partner Dick LeBlond and me trussed up in our neoprene waders, bouncing along in a Russian-made jeep toward the sun sinking behind the mountains beyond the Chilean border to the west.

So there I stood, numbed by traveling the length of two continents, casting blindly into alien water enshrouded by darkness. Strange bird sounds rose from the woods behind us. Even the stars were confusing. Orion stood upside down somewhere near the horizon, while the unfamiliar dimensions of the Southern Cross sprawled across the zenith of the sky overhead—good conditions for the overly literate mind to wander.

Which is how I arrive at blaming a dead English poet for my failure to hook the first fish. Tom and Dick were upstream, arrayed along the head of the pool, scarcely visible against the evening's last light reflected by the legendary Rio Grande. I had taken a good measure of the run in front of me and was at least casting without hanging up on the opposite bank. Beyond that, I could not tell what the fly was doing, and given the inherent mysticism involved in the pursuit of anadromous fish, it was easy enough to become sidetracked by the tenuous thread of circumstances connecting this literal end of the world with the wellsprings of our own culture. Of course, that's when the fish took the fly. By the time I realized what was happening it had already happened, then the line was dead and the river ran cold and dark and there was nothing to do but salute my own inattention with some loud and decidedly nonliterate expletives.

"What was that all about?" Dick called downstream.

"I missed a fish."

Then Dick's voice rose in inarticulate excitement, punctuated by the sound of a fly reel yielding line under protest. Something substantial splashed in the darkness right in front of me. I stumbled back toward shore to give Dick and his fish the run of the pool. It was difficult to follow the course of the struggle in the darkness, but we could hear the fish as it rose and fell and see the rod tip pumping against the glow in the western sky. Finally, Dick had the fish at bay in the shallows, where Tom's flashlight revealed the chrome-bright outline of an eight-pound sea-run brown, fresh from the cold Atlantic.

There aren't a lot of gamefish worth traveling halfway around the world to find, but even in the pale beam of the artificial light, there was no doubt that this was one of them.

Ever since Charles Darwin's seminal voyage aboard the *Beagle*, naturalists have been fascinated by the fauna of Tierra del Fuego. This is a land of natural paradoxes, of penguins and parrots, austere landscapes and vivid plumage. The morning after our arrival, I watched a flock of flamingos glide down the river while a giant Andean condor rode the wind currents far overhead. A herd of *guanacos* loped along beside us, oversized llamas the size of spike elk. I felt what Darwin himself must have felt: a yielding to the relentless spell of the place. I was hooked.

The arrival of the Old World brown trout in this foreign land is a testimonial to two of our own species' strongest impulses: enthusiasm for sport and the urge to meddle. Just after the turn of the century, elements of Argentina's expatriate British community decided that their adopted country's inland waters needed some real gamefish. They hired an American biologist, who began his project by shipping a million whitefish eggs to Argentina's pristine waters. Honest. The whitefish didn't survive, thank God, but subsequent transplants of rainbows and brook trout thrived, largely by virtue of their ability to devour the less competitive indigenous fish population. All the waters of this brave new world needed now was some browns.

Early attempts to introduce brown trout to Argentina failed, but in 1930, stock obtained from Chile (by way of the United States, from their ultimate origins in the British Isles) began to thrive in Patagonia. An Anglo-Argentine named John Goodall accepted the mandate to introduce browns to Tierra del Fuego like a mission from God, which is fortunate, for a lesser degree of determination probably would not have been sufficient to get the job done. Once established in the Land of Fire, the browns did more than flourish. They returned to the sea, becoming the *plateados* of legend in the process.

Of course, the urge to mess with nature always comes at a price, and that price is usually exaggerated in isolated, fragile ecosystems. A few years back, some misguided soul on the Chilean side of the island's arbitrary political border decided that what Tierra del Fuego really needed was a few good rabbits. He raised some, which promptly escaped and set about doing the one thing that rabbits do well. Soon the rabbits overran the landscape. No problem, someone else suggested. We'll just haul some Patagonian foxes across the Strait from the mainland. The foxes solved the rabbit problem in short order, and then went to work on the island's ground-nesting birds. And that, according to our Fuegan hosts, was why little gray foxes were perpetually flitting away at the edges of our vision and why the island's waterfowl population was now a shadow of its former self (although I should note that there were still more than enough ashy-headed geese overhead at all times to make me long hopelessly for my double).

And what of those browns gone wild? What native cultures did they overwhelm? On the mainland of Argentina, there is a move afoot to restore the indigenous fish populations in certain drainages. I suspect that politics on the part of the Argentines are involved, a post–Falklands War resentment that even their bloody fish have been bested by agents of the British Empire. As a naturalist at least, I can sympathize. But as I remember the brilliant, muscular outline of Dick's fish revealed in the flashlight beam, I am also quite willing to make a selfish, imperialist, biologically suspect value judgement:

I am glad the sea-run browns are here.

The morning sun has risen. The light reminds me of Alaska, the way it seems to make the landscape glow from within. We are strung out along a grand sweep in the river known as the Cut-Bank Pool. No one is more ready for the appearance of the *plateados* than me.

The conventional wisdom here calls for large attractor patterns in the pursuit of sea-run browns: Woolly Buggers, Popsicles, Egg-Sucking Leeches. No one ever suggested this would be pretty. Contrary to the end, I am fishing a sparse Atlantic salmon pattern of some kind just because it feels like the right thing to do. Once again, literature almost undoes me.

This time, Shakespeare himself is to blame. More scholarly evidence suggests that Magellan's own description of the area's indigenous people provided the Bard with his model for Caliban, *The Tempest*'s savage. The same description may have influenced Swift's depiction of the giants of Brobdingnag in *Gulliver's Travels*. How is it, I wonder as the Rio Grande licks its way around my thighs, that a land this remote could cast such an influence over several centuries' worth of my own culture's literature? That is just the sort of question that can consume dreamers like me when we should be busy fishing.

The previous evening's miss must have taught me something, however. This time when the fly hesitates, my rod hand strikes like a cobra.

The hell with Shakespeare and the rest; all of a sudden I've got an eight-pound brown turning cartwheels in the sun, throwing bouquets of glistening water droplets back across the river into my face. The reason for Dick's shameless whooping the previous night becomes clear. These fish are hot, the way only fish from the sea can ever be. Even with my seven-weight rod, it is difficult to imagine what I would do with a twenty-pounder.

The Rio Grande is a user-friendly river, however, with open shoulders and few obstructions in the water. The fish orbits the pool once, twice, and then yields at last to the pressure of the rod. Beached gently in the shallows, this brown is as bright as a polished mirror in the sun, with only a few inky freckles scattered along its back to punctuate its perfect sheen. Never has the homology between the brown trout and Atlantic salmon been more apparent.

Downstream, Dick holds his rod high above his head as he backs out of the water and another brilliant silver fish pirouettes in the morning sun. In the days ahead, we will discover that such multiple hookups are not uncommon. The *plateados* are not randomly distributed, and when you find one, you often find more.

Meanwhile, I have suddenly got my hands full, with journalistic impressions to absorb as well as all sorts of things to do with the camera. Somehow, though, I just can't take my eyes off the fish lying in the water in front of me. As soon as I reach down and twist the fly from its jaw, it rockets back into the current as if its battle with my fly rod never took place. I stare wistfully at the emptiness in the water left by its departure. Where did it come from? Where is it going? All the relevant biology remains a mystery.

I only know that it has been rare good fortune to have shared a few minutes of its company along the way.

There are two basic cultural responses to geographic isolation and hardship. The first calls for denial and the deliberate embrace of asceticism, often fueled by the belief that the next world will no doubt be an improvement on this one. Fortunately, the people of Tierra del Fuego have come down strongly in favor of Plan B, which is based on the belief that the more fun you have, the less all the rest of it is likely to matter. In the Fuegans' case, this means of adapting translates into tremendous enthusiasm for all things sporting and lots of great food and drink, especially prime beef, lamb, and red wine, all of which are consumed in Rabelaisian quantities upon the flimsiest excuse.

Which is why Dick and I are beginning our final day on the Rio Grande a bit under the weather. Teddy MacKay, the delightful Scottish-Argentine whose family has operated the Estancia San Jose for three generations, dropped by the night before with a freshly butchered lamb. Pierre, Tom's Argentine partner, grilled the lamb and uncorked a bottle or two, and we all sat around until three in the morning debating topics as diverse as the Meaning of Art and the propriety of stoning anadromous fish from difficult lies. (The latter earned a split decision, by the way; I will not embarrass any of the discussion's participants by recording a rollcall vote.)

So here I stand with the Rio Grande curling its way around my legs once again, its clear waters indifferent to the discomfort in my head, where the remains of the merlot are making a noise like two *guanacos* mating. Downstream, Tom Brady is apologizing for the slow fishing and the fact that we have yet to locate any of the truly huge *plateados* for which the river is famous. Uncharacteristically, I have kept track; in four days of fishing, Dick and I have hooked twenty-nine sea-runs and landed most of them. The smallest of these trout weighed six pounds. Back home in Montana that would be the brown of the season, and almost anywhere else it would be the brown of a lifetime. Clearly, no apologies about the fishing are in order.

And yet there is still one matter I want to settle here. Accustomed as we are to anadromous fish on the fly, both Dick and I can appreciate the mint-bright condition of the trout we have been taking, the silvery iridescence that promises recent arrival from the sea and all the vigor that implies. But I have seen pictures of sea-run browns that have reverted to their true colors after spending some time in fresh water. While these trout may not appeal to the cult of the bright sea-run fish, they look like brown trout, and no fish that swims is as visually compelling as a truly large brown. I don't want to leave without seeing one.

We are back at the Cut-Bank Pool. I am working the riffle at the head of the run, where I have taken half a dozen fish from the fast water in the past two days. Tom is fifty yards below me now, while Dick is casting something big and awful into the still waters near the tail-out. Today, it is Dick who shouts first. I glance downstream to see him braced against the current and a fish, his fly rod bent down toward the water at a perilous angle. The airspace above the river stays empty as whatever Dick has a hold of bores its way sullenly into the deepest reaches of the run. This fish is clearly unlike all the others. I reel in my line, back out of the water, and start down the bank to watch the show.

Dick is way down in his backing and there is not one thing he can do about it. The fish sulks out in the current without regard to pressure from the rod. Tom suggests with prescience that the fish fights like a large male that has been in fresh water for awhile. A specific determination settles over all three of us. We must at least *see* this fish.

Finally, Dick's quarry leaves its defensive position next to the opposite bank and starts downstream toward the distant sea. When Dick manages to turn it, the contested part of the affair is all but done. After several more minutes of back-and-forth denouement, the fish lies panting beside the shore for us to examine, and it is clear that my final wish has been granted.

For unlike the polished-metal specimens we have taken earlier, this fish is unequivocally a brown trout, all fourteen pounds' worth, with yellow flanks and dime-sized spots of red and black and a sullen, undershot jaw. This is the *oro* to complement the sea-fresh *plata*, a fish that could have come right out of my favorite Montana spring creek, except for being about five sizes too large. The three of us stand around and gawk as the fish lets the soothing water of the Rio Grande run easily through its gills. Tom was right: The fish is a male and it has been in the river for awhile, but I am glad of it, fresh sea-run fish be damned.

It all goes so fast, the time we spend in special places. I have been back home less then a month and already my memory is playing tricks. The *guanacos*, the nattering flocks of ibis, Teddy MacKay's improbable Scottish-Castilian-Argentine burr, beef that bursts upon the palate with the complex bouquet of a good claret—it all seems dreamlike now, even the fish. Especially the fish.

I have my slides, but they seem insubstantial somehow, as if nothing there could truly be recorded with such facility. I have my trip notes, but writing is always a pale imitation of the real thing when special places are involved, and even now I feel that I'm struggling more than usual to get it right. Finally, I am left with an understanding, of how this distant end of the earth cast its spell over so many of our own literary predecessors half a world away, and how they struggled to get it right themselves.

Now it's my turn. Perhaps it's that simple after all.

Chapter 16

Death Bunnies and Yankee Flies

 After several months of winter on the prairie, the mere feel of warm salt water on bare feet is nothing less than liberating. As soon as Carl cut the motor and let the skiff ease to a stop, I was over the side just for the pleasure of it—to enjoy the strange conceit that being wet meant being comfortable, to obey my own primal impulse to return to the sea. I ran my hand through the salt water and raised my fingers to my lips. The taste was strange and alluring. Sand eased slowly through my naked toes. I let my eyes drift shut so I could smell the sea more clearly. We had been away from Andros too long, and it felt so good to be back that I just wanted to stand there for a minute and let the feel of the place sink in without hurrying.

With all these sensual impressions fixed at last, it was time to get down to business. The whole notion of getting down to business may seem inappropriate to the relaxed ambience of a Bahamian bonefish expedition, and in a sense it is. I will even admit a touch of guilt at bringing such a driven concept to bear on a morning as innocent as this one. But in a rare fit of disciplined thinking, I had set myself an arbitrary goal for this trip, a standard to provide some sense of structure to those long, deliciously aimless days out on the flats, and it was one that would not be realized easily: I wanted a double-digit bonefish.

Carl had already let it be known that he thought I was a little crazy, a telling judgment from a man who enjoys an islandwide reputation for craziness himself. The problem was not my interest in a big bonefish but the way I wanted to go about it: by wading, off by myself, away from the skiff and Carl and Sheli. It was never my intention to offend anyone, least of all Carl. I just wanted to be alone with the sea and the fish, for reasons of my own.

Carl is a man of firm conviction. Few of his opinions are stronger than his confidence that he knows more about bonefish than anyone, and certainly more than anyone from Montana. He wasn't quite sure how to take my request to be dropped off alone at the edge of the big sand flat in the Middle Bight, although he was perfectly willing to accommodate me. I promised myself I would try to explain my need for solitude to him later, as soon as I could explain it to myself.

"What kind of fly you got there?" Carl asked, as I stood in the water next to the skiff and rigged up.

I finished tying the knot and held it up for his inspection. The fly was a prototype model from my own tying bench that I was anxious to field-test. Reflecting my own long-standing preference for small bonefish flies, the pattern was sparse and delicate. I knew Carl wouldn't like it, and sure enough.

"That looks like some kind of damn Yankee fly to me," Carl said, with as much disdain as he could muster. "Ain't you got a Clouser Minnow or a Gotcha or somethin' *big?*"

I did, and it was too nice a day to argue. I clipped off the fly, which at least had a name now, and replaced it with something twice its size, more in the interest of world peace than because I really thought it would matter to the bonefish. Carl and I agreed on a time to meet, and I said good-bye to Sheli and pushed the skiff back into the channel. Then Carl started the motor and turned in a wide arc and I was alone, just the way I had wanted to be all along.

The wind and the sun were both at my back as I started down the edge of the flat, and the visibility was excellent. It still takes a while to program your eyes for bonefish when you've been away from the flats for a while, and I nearly missed the first school completely. They were already past me when I saw their little push of nervous water, and then the fish themselves became obvious. The cast was an inelegant affair right into the teeth of the breeze, but it was good enough, and the lead fish picked up the fly immediately.

Hooking up the first bonefish after a long absence from the flats always manages to grab right at my heart, like a too-scary rollercoaster ride. One moment the exercise is a purely abstract appeal to shapes in the water that don't even look like fish, and then suddenly I am just standing by, wondering how all that fly line disappeared and whether the demon on the other end ever plans to stop running. There is really nothing else like it anywhere. Think of it as great sex without the complications.

Finally the fish slowed and turned, and there was nothing left to do but begin the long process of reeling it in. I had a good enough look to know that it was no ten-pounder, so it didn't matter much whether I brought it to hand or not. The point is always the strike and the initial wild run; the first measures skill, the second reminds you of nature's power to amaze, and everything else is more like work than any dedicated fly fisher should ever have to admit.

This is an irony I can learn to live with.

Our narrative thus far has raised two questions: Why did I want to be all by myself out there on the Middle Bight? And why was it important that I catch a ten-pound bonefish?

The second question is easier to answer than the first. The sporting life is replete with somewhat arbitrary standards that fall by happy circumstance on round, even units of measure. In the field, for example, the thirty-inch mule deer and the ten-foot bear are the big-game hunter's counterpart of the four-minute mile. The saltwater fly fisher can add two more to the list: *any* permit and a ten-pound bone.

As bonefish grow, they go through a series of stages so distinct that representatives of different size categories scarcely seem members of the same species. Those under two pounds are hardly bonefish at all. Large schools of these smaller fish are common in certain locations, especially in the Yucatán and Belize. They are easy to hook and their sheer numbers evoke a certain amazement, but after awhile, catching *more* of them doesn't really seem to add much to the day.

Three- to six-pound fish will certainly give the angler a fine taste of what the bonefish mystique is all about. They can make reels sing, and when brought to hand they look like gamefish, but after you have caught enough of them you will have trouble remembering them as individuals. By the time bones reach the seven- to nine-pound category, they are the genuine article. These fish can snap leaders on impact and beat up your reel hand. You will want to land each one, and every fish you hook will enjoy your complete attention for as long as you are connected by a fly line—and probably for some time after.

But the ten-pound barrier marks the threshold of truly uncharted territory. These are the six-point bulls of the flats. Landing one requires, in addition to the usual measure of skill and perseverance, an ample bit of luck, for a point will come in every fight with a big bone when you are at its absolute mercy. A ten-pounder's first run commands your attention as quickly as an airplane's stall. To say that ten-pound bones are trophies doesn't begin to do them justice.

And I can't imagine a better place to look for one than Andros Island. Andros enjoys a prominent position in the history of bonefishing. The North Bight is the former home of the once-famous Bang-Bang Club, whose enthusiasts were among the pioneers of sportfishing for bones. Carl's hometown on the Middle Bight was the location of the Andrew Mellon family's winter home. Carl's father was the head fishing guide for the Mellon entourage, which helps explain Carl's own encyclopedic knowledge of local waters. To say that Andros's flats are extensive is to define understatement, and addressing any of them with a fly rod offers the thoughtful angler a unique sense of the sport's history that is some-how lacking in such newly discovered destinations as Christmas Island and Venezuela.

Searching for exceptional representatives of a given species often involves techniques and tactics that differ from those used to take more ordinary specimens, and bonefish are no exception. Just as the whitetail hunter interested in big bucks must often compromise his chance to fill a tag with lesser fare, so must the fly fisher intent on big bones fish differently, and in different places, than the angler whose goal is to hook as many bones as possible without regard to size.

I have fished places that hold more bonefish than Andros, but I have never fished anywhere that offers more chances at truly large fish. During an earlier outing on the North Bight, I saw the biggest bonefish of my life glide by in deep water as I drifted from a flat one afternoon. Its outline was so massive that I initially thought it was a shark. When I finally recognized that yellow bonefish eye staring at me from the crystalline water it was too late to do anything but stare back. Fifteen pounds? Easy. Twenty? Possibly. Carl claims to have taken a twenty-five-pounder on spinning tackle years ago in the Middle Bight. Just knowing that there might be bones of that size in the water you are fishing brings new intensity to every sweep your eyes make across the flats.

Even within a given area, certain spots are often known as big fish hangouts, but these aren't necessarily the places you're likely to see the most fish. Big bones tend to be solitary and favor deeper water than their smaller, more numerous cousins. And some authorities, including the outspoken Carl, feel that big fish require big flies. All this means that the deliberate search for a big bone means a focused approach to the flats. I suppose that's why I constructed the artificial horizon of a double-digit bonefish to guide me through this trip.

It was time to bring things into focus, and I needed all the help I could get.

When you live out on the prairie, you forget how black a tropical night can be. Out on the beach the wind was teasing the palm fronds, but a hundred yards inland the warm air stopped moving and lay tenaciously against the skin. The sky overhead was so dark the stars had trouble shining. Everything around us felt spooky and full of voodoo.

The road to Dig-Dig's was long and straight and uninspiring. Land crabs skittered across the pavement underneath the streetlights and disappeared into the great well of darkness beyond. We walked along quietly, right down the middle of the road, for there was no traffic whatsoever. I waited for Sheli to say something, but she didn't, so I walked on at my own pace and concentrated on the feel of the warm night all around us.

The restaurant was simple and intimate. It served fresh seafood without pretense, and I liked the couple that ran it. He was from the island, she was from Canada, and they seemed as comfortable with their lives as any two people I had met in years. Their contentment with each other and with their circumstances was so complete that you could just sit there and watch it, like a dance or a summer sunset.

Carl met us at the bar, and we all sat down and drank some beer that tasted the way only beer can taste when you are hot and tired and truly thirsty. Carl had promised us a surprise, and when Nelson walked through the door the whole place lit up with the enthusiasm of reunion. It had been years according to the calendar, but it didn't feel as if years had passed as we talked fishing and drank more beer and ate conch fritters. Finally, Nelson reached behind the bar for the telephone and called Edna on Nassau, and Sheli and Edna laughed together longer than it was polite to do on someone else's telephone; but the woman from Canada said it was fine, and I could tell that she meant it.

By the time Sheli and I tumbled out of Dig-Dig's, I was glad that I was walking and not driving. We talked for awhile about how good it had been to see Nelson and talk to Edna, and then lapsed back into silence. I could not keep myself from remembering how the island felt the last time we fished with Nelson. His unexpected appearance had only served to frame my personal discontent. Now I understood why I needed to be alone on the flats and could finally articulate the emptiness, to myself if to no one else. Things were no longer the same, they never would be, and I was going to have to deal with it.

Back at Cargill Creek, the wind was rising from the sea. The air felt cool and comfortable as I lay on top of the sheets and listened to the night unfold, and it was impossible to define the exact moment when I fell asleep.

The next several days confirmed one principle I have long appreciated about flats fishing in the Caribbean: February is not necessarily the best time to do it. Unstable weather can make life difficult then, but winter happens to be the time when I *need* bonefish with that special urgency known only to those who live in cold places.

After two more days of fish in the four- to seven-pound range, I was standing in the skiff's bow one afternoon when I decided to try yet another innovation from my fly book. It was time for a pattern that reflected knowledge culled from years of observation on the flats. It was time for a fly whose very name exuded subtlety, expertise, and finesse. It was time, in other words, for the Death Bunny.

The Death Bunny came to me from its creator, Dale Sexton of Bailey's Fly Shop in Livingston, Montana, by way of mutual friend Steve McGrath, also of Livingston. Steve himself is responsible for yet another revolutionary Andros bonefish pattern, the White-Sex-Death. One can only speculate about what the hell is going on in Livingston that leads to this morbid preoccupation with doom among its anglers. Perhaps that is just what happens when you spend too many Montana winters at the fly-tying bench without going fishing somewhere warm.

The Death Bunny certainly looked like the real thing to me, basically yet another modification of the Nasty Charlie. The mother of all Andros bonefish flies, the Nasty Charlie features a translucent body and bead-chain eyes. Tie in a thin strip of rabbit fur underneath the hook's shank and you've got yourself a Death Bunny, and it certainly suggests something a big bonefish would like to have on the menu. Even the ever-skeptical Carl liked the thing.

As chance would have it, the Death Bunny's first target was the biggest fish I had seen all week. Unfortunately, the encounter also featured one of my worst individual performances of the trip. Somehow, Carl had talked me out of wading, which was why I was fishing from the bow of the skiff. While I can hold my own with Carl spotting fish under most conditions, in deep water he makes me look like I need cataract surgery. This fish was deep, and I didn't see it until Carl yelled at me. The cast was late, I couldn't control my slack line fast enough, and when the fish took the fly I knew at once that I hadn't hooked it solidly. I finally appreciated the size of the fish when it tore past the bow, but I sensed that it wasn't going to matter and it didn't. We parted company on the first run. Ten pounds easy, maybe twelve. *C'est la vie.*

I was philosophical about the loss because I had not come by the fish the way I wanted to and its weight would not have mattered in the end. That sounds like rationalization, but I meant it, and I still do. Real outdoor trophies—a difficult term, but one we seem to be stuck with—depend on process as much as measurement. I wanted a big bonefish, but I didn't want its taking to depend on something someone else had done, which is why I shouldn't have been fishing from the skiff in the first place.

Carl gave me just the right amount of grief over the loss of the fish—not enough to ruin the congenial atmosphere aboard the skiff, but enough to let me know that I should have handled the opportunity better. I could live with that. We let the current carry us on around the next point of land, where the tattered remains of a small vessel lay awkwardly in the mangroves. The boat's design seemed frail and haphazard, as if it never should have been at sea in the first place.

"Haitians, mon," Carl explained as he followed my inquisitive gaze shoreward. "They all dead now. Women and kids, every damn one of them."

Suddenly the flats looked different: the long shimmering miles of bitter water, the isolation, the soft marl that sucked at human footsteps like glue. The sun overhead felt hot and merciless, and all degrees of loss seemed relative. I slid the point of the Death Bunny into the rod's cork handle and sat down, and we drifted off the flat, dropped the motor, and began the long run back toward home.

I spent the last afternoon wading a long sand flat on the Middle Bight. There was nothing left to say to Sheli, and Carl finally seemed comfortable with my need for solitude, so when I bailed out of the skiff this time there wasn't any fidgeting on anyone's part, least of all my own.

Over the next hour I caught several medium-sized bones, but then earned three refusals in a row from fish that should have struck. It was time to change flies. After studying my options, I went back to the Yankee fly, still confident that it was a winner.

Just then I spotted a school of the usual five- to six-pound suspects working their way toward me against the current. As I plotted an intercept, something caught my eye from the direction of the channel running along the edge of the flat. It was a solitary cruising bone, a big one.

The cast fell into the lead-upwind-and-hope category, and the near-perfect result was more a product of luck than skill. The fish turned immediately and darted back and forth over the fly. Finally I felt something soft and heavy on the line, and when I set the hook the whole flat seemed to explode.

The first hurdle in the battle with a big bone is getting the inevitable mess of surplus fly line started on its way through the guides. One wayward loop too many and the fight is over before it begins. By the time I had accomplished this task, the fish was headed for deep water with conviction, and I was in the grip of a sensation one seldom experiences in this era of the catch-and-release ethic. Simply stated, I wanted to land this fish very much, not because I wanted to kill it, but because, well . . . because. We've been through that already.

It takes a lot of fish to spool you when your reel holds nearly two hundred yards of line, but that seemed to be my immediate fate. I fumbled with the drag, and when that didn't work I began to slog across the flat in pursuit. Could a week of fishing really come down to this, the simple disappearance of the object of all that desire? Maybe this fish was meant to teach me something, I thought, as I applied as much pressure as I dared. Maybe this is just what you deserve for bringing all that acquisitiveness to an activity as fundamentally innocent as fly fishing. Maybe.

By the time the first run ended I nearly had the loss of the fish explained away. Metal peeked through the last of the backing on the reel's axle; it had been that close. It takes a long time to reclaim that much line with a single-action fly reel, especially when the process is interrupted regularly by more runs, but finally the fish came to rest at my feet, and I could reach down and touch its sleek iridescent sides and feel its heft cradled gently in my hand.

First I slid the Yankee fly from the fish's lip, to be retired with full honors. Then I retrieved the little brass scale from my belly bag, where it had waited all week for just this moment. The fish rested submissively, the last of its fight expended. All it had to do now was obey the law of gravity for a few seconds before returning to the sea. I held the scale aloft, and as the fish's tail cleared the water I studied the numbers. Nine and a half pounds. Period.

Not one ounce more.

All right. Perhaps there really is a lesson to be learned from all this, a lesson beyond the obvious ones like *set your hook, stupid.* After all, fishing is not a competitive sport and even when competition involves only oneself, its mere presence where it does not belong sets the stage for disappointment. No one should go fishing in order to be disappointed.

On the other hand, raising one's sights can be responsible for some of the best moments in outdoor sport, as long as the process doesn't get out of hand. I still relish the way I needed to land that last fish, and how that need made the whole flat seem intense and urgent. Fishing had not made me feel that way for years, perhaps since childhood, when rods and reels were a means of putting fish in frying pans. It mattered then whether or not you landed what was on the end of the line, in a way hard to reproduce without the intent to draw blood. Say what you will; it could not have been all bad.

And what was the final legacy of those few missing clicks on the scale? No doubt some would frame the matter in terms of failure: a pass dropped in the end zone, a stock purchased just before the market falls, a marriage doomed for reasons neither party can articulate.

I say it sounds more like a great excuse for the best ending in outdoor writing:

To be continued. . . .

Chapter 17

Dream Fish

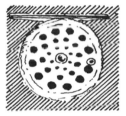 Although one ocean can drown you just as dead as another, no body of water looks so up to the job as the Pacific. Even on a calm day the Pacific is intimidating, no matter what you make of the irony inherent in its name. It makes you feel small and insignificant, like the Milky Way on a starry summer night. Throw in some swells and surf, and our largest ocean can make anyone start looking for high ground. You know, just in case. And nowhere is this uneasy relationship between man and sea uneasier than in its middle, far from the mainland and the apparent sense of security the sheltering continents provide.

The east end of Molokai'i is just such a place. The day I caught the *weke*, the surf had kicked up enough to get the local kids out in the water on their boards, and it looked like so much fun that it was hard to keep my eyes on the road as we drove along the shoreline toward our destination. There wasn't anything fancy going on out there, but that made it all look more genuine somehow, like watching a ballerina unaware of her audience.

Doug and I had been bowhunting boars and axis deer for several days, and we were tired of climbing mountains in the heat. We planned to spend the afternoon with Olga and Lori, snorkeling and trying to catch a Hawaiian bonefish on a fly. The diving part was easy enough to imagine, but the bonefish was another matter. Neither of us had ever heard of anyone doing it on Molokai'i before, at least not on fly tackle.

It's not that Hawaii lacks bonefish. Known locally as *oi'o*, bonefish are an important traditional Hawaiian food source (although it should be noted that it's difficult to find something from the sea that *isn't* a traditional Hawaiian food source). The official state sportfishing record is better than eighteen pounds, which is one hell of a bonefish. The problem is, along the rugged Hawaiian coastline bones spend most of their time in deep water, where sight-casting to them with fly tackle is virtually impossible. Nonetheless, Doug and I were determined to give it a try, motivated more by the spirit of adventure and the need to spend some time in the water than by any conviction that one of us might actually manage to hook a bonefish.

At least we enjoyed the benefit of local knowledge. A year or two earlier, Doug had been bowfishing for *uhu* along a rocky cove when he actually spotted a school of bones in the shallow water that flanked a deep cut angling across the reef. Doug is not one to forget intelligence like that, and he had carefully filed the sighting away for future reference. All he needed to turn it into a genuine fishing expedition was another bonefish fool for company, and now he had one.

We parked along the winding road high above the sea, and set off through the rocky cliffs toward the cove carrying both our fly rods and our snorkeling gear. Across the channel to the south the island of Maui beckoned, with its shoreline resorts glimmering like a mirage in the sun. Why can't I ever do anything the easy way? I wondered, as we worked our way down through the rocks with the waves crashing underneath us. Why can't I go to Hawaii and be a tourist like everyone else, writing postcards and sipping mai-tais and working on my tan?

We finally arrived at the cove to find that we had miscalculated the tide. Sight-casting was impossible, but we had come too far to turn back without saluting the water. We had been snorkeling and spear-fishing with our Hawaiian friends all week, and I knew the water was full of fish, though few of the species are classic fly-rod fare. Besides, there was always the possibility of hooking a bonefish or a *papio* by casting blind, which would be some kind of accomplishment in its own right.

While Olga and Lori donned their snorkeling gear, I rigged my eight-weight rod, tied on a weighted fly, stripped down to my shorts and wading shoes, and slogged into the surf. I slipped several times as I fought through the surge, but then I got my legs under me and continued outward through the waist-deep water next to the channel.

I've never been a technical student of fly casting, but there are days when the mysterious physics of rod and line can make up for a lot of uncertainty on the part of the fish, and this was one of them. A stiff onshore breeze was blowing, but it didn't matter. Everything felt perfectly balanced and harmonious, and the fly shot effortlessly into the teeth of the wind each time I asked it to. Casting felt like an extended *tai chi* exercise, and it didn't matter that I wasn't catching any fish, or even that I didn't know for sure what kind of fish I wasn't catching.

The sea kept rolling into the little cove and knocking me around rudely, but that didn't matter either. It turns out that it isn't necessary to stand upright when casting in the surf. In fact, as long as the weather is warm and you are comfortable in rough water, floundering around in the breakers with a fly rod in your hand has a loopy appeal all its own. It makes you feel intimate with the aquatic environment and, consequently, with your quarry. At least that's what I told myself when a particularly unruly swell picked me up and knocked me ass-over-tea kettle backward toward the beach, fly rod and all.

After half an hour of this carrying-on, however, I was beginning to feel more like flotsam than a fisherman. Then, just as I was about to give up and head back toward shore, the miraculous occurred. Something vital grabbed the fly out in the surge. It was apparent at once that I had hooked something smaller and less traditionally inspiring than a bonefish, but I didn't care. There *were* fish out there, and at least one was the kind that struck flies. I whooped in triumph, but the surf swallowed my voice, and there was no one to share my secret but the sea.

It didn't take long to land the fish—basslike in profile, a foot or so long, with rough scales and dark, vertical purple, black, and crimson stripes along its flanks. A pair of long barbels sprouted from its chin and retracted neatly into grooves along the lower mandible. Although I am no authority on Pacific reef fish, this identified my prize unequivocally. I had caught a goatfish. Who knows? It might even have been some kind of record on fly tackle.

Now I had a decision to make. The obvious thing to do was slide the hook from its lip and throw the fish back in the surf, but it came out of the water with the deer-in-the-headlights look that saltwater species sometimes demonstrate after a hard fight; "releasing" these fish usually amounts to little more than feeding the sharks. Besides, we had spent the whole week with our native Hawaiian friends, and their intense hunter-gatherer instincts were wearing off on all of us. After a moment's consideration, I whacked the fish on the back of the head and slid it into my belly bag for safekeeping.

Tired of the ocean's relentless pounding, I worked my way back toward shore and showed off my fish. Then we all went snorkeling. The surf was far easier to manage while adrift. With no need to keep my feet beneath my center of gravity, I was free to rise and fall with the rhythm of the sea, diverting the energy of each wave into a free ride instead of an ass-kicking. There was probably a lesson to be learned there, about fishing and the sea and God knows what, but I was too busy studying the silent world beneath the waves to waste time on philosophy.

There were plenty of fish out there, but most were even smaller than my goatfish. There were good numbers of large, brilliantly colored *uhu*, but parrot fish are coral-eaters, of no interest to fly fishers. I did see one fighting-sized *papio*, as small trevally of all species are known in Hawaii, but as conventional gamefish go, that was about it. Finally, my gullet reached its quota of salt water and I headed for shore.

Everyone else had already come in. As we toweled down, we compared notes on the fish we had seen, then started to pack our gear for the hike back out to the road. That's when Doug reached into his pocket and discovered he had lost our only set of car keys somewhere out on the reef.

This is not the kind of news one takes lightly at the end of a long day, when good food and drink are beckoning back home. Still, everyone remained calm. Always the optimist, Doug suggested that we put on our masks and go search for the missing keys. Olga and Lori looked at the sea rising and falling in the cove and told us this was crazy, and it was hard to disagree. Doug said that he thought he knew where he might have lost the keys, but the ocean looked so big and the key ring was so small. Secretly I agreed with Lori and Olga, but abandoning Doug to search by himself felt like a breach of honor. I dug my mask and snorkel out of the gear bag and we headed back to the sea.

The current was running harder now, and snorkeling the area where Doug thought he had lost the keys required us to weave our way precariously in and out of the rocks. The rugged bottom was full of cracks and crevices, and the chance of finding the keys seemed almost infinitesimal. Nonetheless, I kept at it, more as a show of mental support for Doug than because of a true conviction that this was anything but a lost cause. Then I came up to clear my mask and heard a commotion in the water beside me, and there was Doug, shouting above the noise of the surf and holding the key ring overhead like the Holy Grail. Surely the gods were smiling on us, for reasons known only to them.

The flood tide of our good fortune carried us all the way home, where sashimi and cold beer were waiting. Then I remembered my goatfish. It was time to do a little fisheries research, and I dug out an appropriate reference book.

It turns out that numerous members of the goatfish family inhabit Hawaiian waters. Mine was a red *weke*, a fish of considerable traditional importance in the islands that is still highly prized on the table. According to Hawaiian folklore, all land animals have counterparts at sea. The red *weke* is one of the esteemed "sea pigs," equivalent to prized pork on the table. Furthermore, the color red is of great ceremonial significance, and red *weke* were often served in this ritual capacity at formal feasts. And to think: I had caught one on a fly.

There was, however, a catch. Some varieties of island goatfish evidently can be hallucinogenic when eaten. They are known as dream *weke*, and consuming one can lead to vivid psychedelic experiences. The details in my source book were too sketchy to determine whether I had a dream *weke* or a regular old *weke* sitting in the refrigerator. The virtues of catch-and-release never seemed clearer, but it was too late for that now.

I put down my book and explained the problem to Doug. "Call Kimo," he suggested. "He'll know what to do."

I called Kimo and described both the fish and my dilemma to him. "Don't eat the brains," he advised.

"I wasn't planning on it," I assured him.

"It sounds like a good fish to me," he said. "I'd eat it."

"Thanks," I said. Of course Kimo is known for his willingness to eat almost anything from the sea, and his friends will understand why this advice somehow failed to reassure me.

I went to the refrigerator. There was the fish. I took it to the sink and scaled it carefully. The flesh felt firm and inviting. It was my fish; I had killed it and I was going to eat it. I opened a beer and turned a front burner on the stove to medium heat. The beer felt cool and reassuring, a perfect counterpoint to the warm air hanging tenaciously inside the kitchen.

For me, cooking is almost always a relaxing, contemplative experience, especially when I'm cooking something I have caught or shot myself. I watched a dollop of butter melt inside the skillet and turned down the heat. I was grating some ginger over the pan when Olga walked into the kitchen with a book in her hand. According to *her* reference, the phenomenon of the psychedelic goatfish was most frequently noted in the waters near Molokaʻi during the month of August. That was us. Furthermore, her book did not use the term dream *weke*. According to Hawaiian legend, she explained, the goatfish acquired its capacity to enchant on the nearby island of Lanai, when Pahulu, chief of evil spirits, was slain by an adversary and fell into the sea from which he returned in the form of the *nightmare weke*. Oh. Why couldn't I have caught something more conventional, or slid this fish back into the sea when I had the chance?

Everyone had gathered in the kitchen by now. I added soy sauce to the pan, followed by a pinch of sugar. With all the ingredients blended together, I turned up the heat again, and just as the butter started to smoke slid the *weke* into the pan. Just three or four minutes on each side, and it looked inviting in its sauce, like something in a specialty seafood restaurant.

Lori and Olga, with last-minute reservations, suggested I stick to the fresh ahi we had been enjoying. I studied my fish the way a diver studies the water beneath a high board. I thought of the lost keys on the reef, whose recovery seemed a propitious omen if ever there was one. And after surviving Berkeley in the sixties, was I really going to turn tail and run from a hallucinogenic fish the size of my hand? No. Make that hell no.

I picked up my chopsticks and started to eat, and the tender white meat fell easily away from the bone. The fish was absolutely delicious, and the rich sauce complemented its taste perfectly. I offered everyone else a bite, but there were no takers. I started to pick the cheeks out of the gill covers, but I remembered Kimo's admonition and decided I could leave that end of the fish alone without sacrificing any moral integrity.

It had been a long day and we were tired. Doug and Olga and Lori cleaned up the rest of the *ahi* while I finished off my dream fish and washed it down with one last swallow of beer. Then we all trooped off to bed, where I lay on top of the covers, listened to the wind outside the lanai, and waited for Pahulu and the world of dreams to overtake me.

The purpose of this recounting is not to suggest serious fly-rod expeditions in search of goatfish or another tedious chapter in the annals of psycho-pharmacology, but to remind us just how arbitrary the concept of sport can become if we let it. I often marvel at the near-religious conviction with which so many fly fishers approach the bonefish flats. Not that there's anything wrong with bonefish, but there are so many other things out there in the sea to intrigue us if we would only give them a chance. Salt water means variety, and it seems a shame not to sample it just because of someone else's notion of a fixed agenda.

Remember that, just a few years ago, bonefish were regarded as saltwater suckers, and no one thought it was possible to catch a permit on a fly. (Some of us still don't, but that's another story.) It took pioneers to discover the pleasures these species can offer on the end of a fly line, and they probably endured their share of raised eyebrows and behind-the-back sneers in the process. Now look how far we've come thanks to their efforts.

I'm sure there are lots of sleeper species out there somewhere in the sea, waiting to excite adventuresome anglers willing to do what has to be done to discover them. I am also sure, to be quite honest, that the dream *weke* isn't one of them. Small fish that fight no better than you'd expect them to, they look like overdressed crappies with whiskers, and no amount of romantic spin-doctoring can change these basic facts. As for their hallucinogenic qualities, let's just say that the reputation of the peyote button and magic mushroom should remain secure. Of course, I didn't eat my *weke*'s head, an oversight that boils down to smart thinking or chickening out, depending on how you feel about that sort of thing. Maybe next time I'll read Castenada before dinner and take the exploration one step farther.

For I am going back to that rocky cove someday, and I'm taking my fly rod with me when I go. It's not that I really expect to catch an *oi'o* out there, although the thought of doing so is certainly exciting enough. It's the other fish that really intrigue me —those that no one else knows or imagines, the ones that lurk at the edge of the dark water while anglers go about their business according to schedule.

Someone must find and speak for them, and then they can make us all dream at night.

Chapter 18

The Absence of
Sharks

Saturday. TACA, the principal airline serving the nation of Belize, operates on island time. Unfortunately, the world's international air transport system adheres to a more structured schedule, which is why Ray and Joe and Jenny and I are sitting in a dimly lit bar in Belize City instead of oiling our fly reels at the edge of the reef in preparation for an early-morning assault on the flats. The kids are drinking Coke. Ray and I are drinking beer, which the heat is turning to sweat by the cupful. Our connections to the fishing village that is our final destination are sounding more and more tenuous by the minute, but nobody really cares anymore. We are on vacation, and we are beginning to operate on island time ourselves.

Belize has changed. Ray and I have been coming here for years, since before the kids were even born, for bonefish and tarpon and the reef. In the beginning there was no tourist presence, and the place offered a sort of cultural anonymity that provided a perfect complement to its natural splendor. Now there are Americans everywhere, God help us, and they have brought with them a curious mixture of the best and the worst our generation has to offer: regard for the out-of-doors smothered in a stifling sense of the politically correct. Nowadays even fly rods draw suspicious stares from the ecotourists, never mind the spears and Hawaiian slings.

I have two missions on this trip. The first is one of my Caribbean standards: catch a permit on a fly. I've been trying to do this for so long it has become an epic comedy of sorts. Catching a permit is something that I no longer seriously think I'm going to do. It's just a reason to go, and a damn good one at that.

My second mission is to patch up some loose ends with Jenny. She is a mature almost-thirteen, an awkward age under the best of circumstances, and the last year hasn't been the best for either of us. She is starting to talk about boys more than horses, never a good sign at this age, and we are clearly overdue for the sort of parental reckoning best served up in wild places.

Everyone is tired after too many hours in airports. I glance across the table at my daughter, at once resolute and vulnerable, and then at the press of our own countrymen crowded around the hotel bar. Finally, I understand. It is not just the tourists that have made Belize different. Of my dozen trips here, this is the first without Jenny's mother.

Oh, man. I call for another Belikan. Somewhere out there in the dark tropical night, the wild reef beckons. I wonder if I'll get there soon enough.

Monday. The tide is wrong for wading the flats, so we are trolling the blue water outside the reef with lust in our hearts.

Our first rule for taking kids fishing in salt water is that the kids should catch some fish, *kids* in this case being loosely defined as anyone under the age of fifty. This principle correlates nicely with our second rule, which is that dinner should always be something we have taken from the sea. I enjoy the second rule every bit as much as the first, because I love to eat fresh fish and because I abhor the self-righteousness with which some have elevated catch-and-release from management tool to divine commandment, even if biologically unwarranted. Let's face facts: It's *good* to whack a fish over the head from time to time, especially if the fish is a snapper destined for the grill and ultimately for your plate.

Derek is at the helm. Although renowned as a permit guide, he's no snob. The fact is, Derek likes fishing for just about anything, which makes him right at home in our program. Joe is trolling a tube lure along the surface while Jenny is dragging a truly monstrous deep-diving plug just above the coral heads. The sun gazes down as pelicans wheel overhead. The morning's pace feels just right to me. The permit can wait. I may not be running on island time yet, but I'm getting close.

Then Jenny's rod tip goes down so abruptly it looks like we'll lose the rod or Jenny or both. Everyone is up, on point with curiosity; only the sea, with the indefinite upper end to the size of its fish, can do that to you. Unseen, the fish bores down relentlessly toward the security of the reef below. Then the line fouls on a coral head and all our speculation about its identity seems academic.

Jenny pumps angrily at the deadweight on the other end of the line. I cradle my arms around her, place my hands on the rod, and let the line go nearly slack. After a minute's wait, something soft and vital declares itself. I get my shoulders into it and horse the fish a dozen feet off the bottom before placing the rod back in Jenny's hands. From then on, the fight is manageable.

It turns out to be a twenty-pound red grouper, just what we need for the icebox during the days ahead. As it comes over the side, the fish looks like sashimi, fillets, fish sandwiches; I just can't help myself. Everyone is happy, a development that in a fit of misguided desperation I nearly spoil with a quiet parable in the bow about groupers in coral and fathers and daughters working together to solve their problems.

"Oh, Dad," Jenny interrupts. "Let's just go fishing."

To which suggestion I can offer no rebuttal.

Wednesday. The water progresses through a spectrum of color as it falls away from the narrow flat, from pale yellow through turquoise to the impenetrable cobalt blue of the sea. The tide is right and the wind has died at last. At my request, Derek has dropped me off alone at the head of this meandering splinter of sand and coral. Jenny has spent the morning being contrary, secure in the adolescent certainty that she knows everything there is to know. I can't take it anymore, to put it simply. It's time to work out on some permit.

My personal quest for a permit on a fly has acquired a fairy tale absurdity. Too many permit have told me in so many words to give it up. It's not the fish but the process that counts now, the visual excitement of tails glistening in the sun and the technical challenge of the presentation, even though I know every cast I make is doomed to futility. For me, fly fishing for permit has become more Zen exercise than sport.

The air is heavy, the sea beneath it almost unnaturally still. A gang of jacks chases a school of baitfish up onto the seaward edge of the flat, but

I ignore them. If you're going to commit yourself to not catching permit, you had better be willing to commit yourself totally.

Then the tails appear, waving high above the glassy surface nearly eighty yards away down the flat. There are at least three of them. They are rising up and down regularly as they feed, and they don't seem to be going anywhere. Oh no, I think. Here we go again.

There is nothing to do but fix their position and wade on down the line. Thirty yards from my quarry, I pull the crab fly from the hook-keeper and begin to work out line overhead. Intent on something tasty beneath them, the fish are hardly spooky, and I wade closer than necessary to guarantee an accurate cast. The distance between each tail tip and dorsal fin seems to go on forever, and now that I can see the fish themselves, it's obvious that all three are big enough to give anyone the pitter-patters.

I wait until I've got all three fish accounted for, then drop the fly just ahead of them and twitch it seductively past their field of vision. Nothing happens. (Why doesn't this surprise me?) Another cast, a little slower retrieve, and a quick drop of the fly to the bottom produces the same result. The fly is a carefully crafted McCrab, the world's most effective permit pattern, a spitting image of the little tan *congrejos* that have been scurrying away underfoot ever since I started down the flat. My first two presentations have been perfect, as are a dozen more. The permit, all seventy-odd collective pounds of them, couldn't care less. Their tails appear and disappear, graceful and insolent, the perfect punishment for some uncertain sin.

Finally, I lose track of one of the fish and spook it with the line and they are gone, the way mirages disappear from the road on hot days when you close within a critical distance. I reel in slowly and stare at the empty sea, resisting the urge to read more meaning into this than the situation really demands. They are just being permit. I am just being a permit fisherman. No further explanation is available, and fortunately, none is required.

There aren't a lot of bonefish along this part of the reef, but twenty minutes later I take my eyes off the surface where the permit tails should be and look down into the water and there they are, a dozen green shapes tacking back and forth easily into the gentle flow across the flat. Like the permit earlier, they aren't really going anywhere, which gives me time to clip off the McCrab and substitute a real bonefish pattern.

These fish are eager, in profound contrast to the permit, and the fly barely hits the water before I'm hooked up and the whole school of bones is headed for the deep. None of the fish looked particularly big, and the one I've hooked feels like it only weighs about three pounds, but I'm still happy as a hog in slop because I've got an actual fish on my line. The hell with permit; this is real fishing.

Coral flats pose technical problems of their own. Even with smaller bonefish, there's a trick to keeping your line from fouling during that first wonderful run. The trick consists of keeping your rod tip high and being very lucky. So far, so good. I've got the fish turned around within the first third of my backing, and when it tears back past me across the white sand, damned if it still doesn't have the whole school tagging along. After the permit fiasco, this is simply wonderful. I've not only hooked one fish; I've hooked the whole lot of them.

Suddenly there is a great commotion right in front of me that suggests at once some kind of disaster. The line goes dead but not slack, and the school of bonefish streaks away over the exposed coral in such a state of panic that some come right out of the water. Then the 'cuda appears in a sudden swirl right at my feet. Small barracuda look like big pickerel; big ones look like dragons. This is a big one.

I strip in the line and lift the remains of my catch above the water. The bonefish is nothing but head and torso, gasping stupidly in the sunlight, bewildered by the sudden disappearance of its other half. The wound that killed it is surgically precise and merciless. This could have been your foot, the perfectly beveled cut seems to suggest. This could have been your wrist.

Meanwhile, the barracuda just will not go away, as if it knows it has been short-changed by half a bonefish. In the clear, shallow water, the 'cuda is all piercing eye and vicious undershot jaw, and every time it swirls in front of me I cannot help thinking that, as an African friend once said of a black mamba, it looks just like the devil. I'm torn by conflicting impulses toward the 'cuda: to catch it, to kill it, to turn around and walk away before this adventure gets out of hand. Finally, I settle for throwing what's left of the bonefish at the barracuda's head and retreating down the flat, proving nothing but my own petulance in the process.

And so the sea has not been generous this morning, first refusing to give and then taking back what it had so reluctantly given. Even so, I harbor no grudges. We are sportsmen here, not accountants or score-keepers. The tide will rise again tomorrow. Fool that I am, I'll be there waiting for it.

Saturday. Of all the tiny cays we have visited, this is the first to support a permanent residence, and it's a surprisingly luxurious one at that. Derek has already alerted me to the identity of the owner, and it's such an incongruous, juicy piece of gossip that I can't wait to spring it on Jenny, infatuated as she is with rock 'n' roll.

"Hey, Jenny," I ask, as we cruise past the deserted dock and drop anchor behind the adjoining reef. "Know whose place that is?"

"Whose?"

"Mick Jagger's!"

"Who's Mick Jagger?"

Oh, God, can it really have come to this? I hand Jenny her mask and fins and then slide into my own. When I roll over the gunwale and into the receptive sea, it is with the hope that I can somehow leave the yawning gulf of generations and my own middle age behind me.

I've never understood why spear-fishing gets so little attention in the sporting literature. It is a marvelous marriage of hunting, fishing, and exercise, all served up in some of the most glorious settings the outdoors has to offer. Like all the things we do, it can be done wrong, so there are rules to keep it from crossing the line between sport and exploitation: no SCUBA, no mechanical spear-guns, no shooting docile reef fish. Taken on these terms, it offers a perfect interlude between rounds of humiliation at the hands of the permit.

Jenny has taken to snorkeling the reef like a natural. It's no surprise really, since she is an athletic and adventurous kid. And so we set off together along the coral heads with one spear and sling between us and the silent, vivid world of the reef sliding easily along beneath us like a dream.

We have finally eaten our way through Jenny's grouper, but I'm not really hunting today, even when it's my turn to carry the spear. Young Joe has become a master of this game. I know he'll put something good in the icebox for dinner tonight, which frees me from some of my own hunter-gatherer instincts. Jenny is another matter. She dives toward a patch of sand and surfaces with a live conch, which she holds aloft like a trophy. Conch fritters are the staple appetizer from my makeshift kitchen in the village, but neither of us feels like swimming all the way back to the boat with this one. We discuss our options while bobbing about on the waves, our voices and features contorted comically by our masks. Then Jenny drops the conch and we press our faces back down underwater and watch together as it descends in slow motion toward its original resting place.

Slowly, we move on toward the edge of the reef. The fish are bigger here, but I still don't feel like a hunter. It is enough to float along on the current and feel the cool surge of blue water reach out and tease us. The challenge here is to keep yourself from feeling like bait. Years ago, a Belizean friend offered a memorable bit of wisdom on the subject. Don't look for sharks down there, he told me solemnly. Why not? I wondered. Because, he explained, if you look for them, you will see them, and then you will stop having a good time.

And so I drift lazily along, not looking for sharks and waiting for a glimpse of a grouper big enough to make me feel like a predator again. Suddenly there is a commotion on the surface beside me. It is Jenny. A wave has broken over the top of her snorkel and she has taken in a mighty shot of seawater. Graceful no longer, she is doing the vertical dog paddle and getting nowhere in the process.

I swim swiftly to her side, whereupon she does what all people do when they are convinced that they are drowning, which is to try to climb their rescuer like a tree. Suddenly I remember what teaching her to swim was like, but she isn't three years old anymore, and I'm not thirty. Besides, she's got me in a headlock amply motivated by panic, and despite a lifetime at ease in the water, I realize for the first time just how far out in the sea we really are.

I take a gulp of air and let myself slide down into the water. She instinctively lets go and struggles to the surface gagging and sputtering, her features contorted and her mask askew. Then I come up behind her and take control, laying her supine across my outstretched arms and encouraging her to breathe slowly and surely. Common sense returns at last. I ease the mask away from her face. Finally, she blows two great streamers of saline snot from her nostrils and the crisis passes.

"I'm okay now," she says at last.

"I know," I tell her.

"Thanks, Dad."

For once, neither of us is in a hurry to do other things. We remain together for as long as you can imagine, treading water, soaking up sun, a parent and a child alone together in the middle of a vast, indifferent sea.

Monday. The road home always feels longer somehow. We are sitting in the Houston airport, tanned and pleasantly bedraggled, isolated by the sudden hurry of our own culture. Right in front of us, three men in suits are comparing cellular telephones, arguing the merits of one model over another with no indication whatsoever that they might be kidding. This much is certain: We are on island time no longer.

In the world of Disney endings, the outcomes would all be predictable. I would catch the permit, Jenny would experience a catharsis of filial understanding, and everyone would live happily ever after. Our own world, however, remains full of complications, with hard choices lurking around every corner. Permit or bones? Fish or dive? Mom or Dad?

My Belizean friend was right about one thing. There really are sharks just beyond the edge of the reef, and if you stare out into the blue water long enough, you're eventually going to see them.

Whether that is good or bad is another matter. Perhaps sport does nothing more in the final analysis than provide a mechanism to promote the suspension of our own unhappy belief. In that case, we are all to be congratulated, for at least we have invented a construct that works.

They are paging our flight. We rise together and set off once more into the world of sharks and barracuda, blue water and fragile dreams.

Chapter 19

Christmas Past

The sun was sliding toward the western horizon where the vast crescent of the Pacific waited patiently to receive it. Water spread away forever in front of us; a low flat arc of scrub brush coiled its way behind our backs. There were no landmarks anywhere. A frigate bird towered overhead as still as death, a dark image from a Bergman movie hanging by magic from an indifferent sky. Scarcely deeper than our ankles, the water felt as warm and still as I had ever known it.

This was a new flat, and we had no idea what to expect from it. There were no defining features at all, and I felt like a lost pawn on an empty chessboard. The light was all wrong anyway, and I was just about to yell across the water to Dick and suggest a timely retreat when the first tail appeared high above the blood-red sea.

The sight of tails arouses excitement above and beyond all other visual cues to the presence of bonefish. I have considered invoking elaborate sexual metaphors to explain this phenomenon and decided to pass, no doubt for the good of us all. And it's not just that tailing bonefish are feeding bonefish, for tailing fish can be quite selective and difficult to catch. One reason bonefish fools get all flustered when tails appear above the water derives from basic anatomy. Bonefish have big tails, and tailing bones almost always look several sizes larger than they eventually prove to be. Coupled with the shimmery elegance of the tail waving

169

above the waterline, this simple illusion explains my sudden attack of sweaty palms. At first glance, the fish looked as if it would weigh eight or nine pounds, when in fact it was scarcely half that size.

What breeze remained blew steadily at my back, and the cast was nothing more than a chip shot. The take was immediate, soft, and satisfying. I coaxed the loose loops of line through the lower guide and stretched the rod tip as high as I could make it go to keep from fouling on the coral, and then the fish was off on a long sweeping run toward the sea.

Plainly delighted to learn that the flat wasn't barren after all, Dick shouted encouragement across the shallows. The fish ran hard and true until it had nothing more to run with, and then it presented me with the profoundly anticlimactic chore of reeling it in. It managed one more little sizzle of protest on the way, then gave up and came about like a tired dog on a leash.

All right; it didn't weigh eight pounds. I unfurled the tail and confirmed once more how much larger it looked than the rest of the bonefish, but I didn't care, not in the end. The fish was still chunky and marvelous, with subtle vertical stripes across its back and a tenacious layer of slime along its flanks just ready to curdle on my hands. This fish would do. When things are going well, the one you've just caught always does.

By the time I released the fish and stood up, I could see Dick casting intently to targets of his own. Another tail appeared in front of me, but as I started to work my line overhead I was distracted by the appearance of still another fish, and then another. I held my fire, studied the surface of the water sweeping away before me, and realized that bonefish had appeared everywhere as suddenly as mushrooms on a wet lawn. Waves of tailing bonefish extended as far ahead as I could see into the afternoon sun's orange glow, so many it was impossible to estimate their numbers.

For a moment I stood and enjoyed the simple spectacle of it all. Then my predatory instincts took over. I cast to the nearest fish, and hooked it at once. As it tore off across the flat with my fly line hissing angrily behind, tails vanished along its route of retreat only to reappear as soon as the disturbance passed. Clearly, these fish were in a feeding mode that wasn't about to yield to common sense.

Over on his side of the flat, Dick was shouting something inarticulate as he hooked another fish. By the time I began to reclaim my own line, I had already located my next target. As soon as I released the second fish, I cast toward the third and hooked it as quickly as I had hooked the other two. More bonefish continued to appear all around me. Matters were getting out of control.

I regard myself as a reasonably contemplative outdoorsman, and spend my share of time in the field appreciating aesthetics and The Meaning Of It All. However, there come times when it's best to forget all about that crap and just have at it in the best tradition of Lord Ripon. Bonefish flats offer few opportunities to indulge in gluttony, and I know enough to take advantage of them when they do.

I tried concentrating on big fish, but they all looked to weigh from three to five pounds. The thing to do seemed to be to catch as many as possible before the tide changed or the sun went down. And that's just what we did.

I don't know how many we caught, but it was an awful lot of bonefish. I suppose we could be criticized for mindlessly hammering the resource, except that mindlessly hammering the resource sometimes is just what fly fishing is all about. Catching bonefish has no point, after all, other than its own process, which we exercised to the fullest, until the sun settled into the distant sea and we turned and slogged our way back toward the shoreline in the dark.

Ordinarily, memorable fishing leaves behind the impression that I have done something to the fish, but this time I left the water with the feeling that they had done something to me—exhausted me with their numbers, overwhelmed me with their enthusiasm for the fly, reminded me how small people really are in comparison to the sea. Dick agreed; neither of us had ever seen anything quite like it. My shoulder hurt. My backing had worn a groove in my index finger that throbbed from the sting of the salt water. Worn marl crunched between my feet and wading shoes, and I was thankful that we didn't have to walk any farther than we did.

And yet there were no regrets. In fact, neither of us would have missed it for the world.

Leave it to bonefish to do what coconuts, bird shit, war, and the detonation of nuclear devices tried and failed to do for centuries: make Christmas Island an attractive landfall for human visitors.

The island has always been out of the loop of human affairs, despite being one of the largest atolls in the Pacific. To the region's early Polynesian explorers, it was known as *Abakiroro*, the faraway island,

171

and archaeological evidence suggests only transient visitation by Polynesian explorers.

The western discovery of Christmas Island accrues to none other than the intrepid Captain James Cook, the man we last saw struggling to float his flagship off a sandbar in the treacherous Alaska inlet that now bears his name. Six months later, in December 1777, he brought his ships cautiously about into the lee of a large horseshoe-shaped atoll just north of the equator, once again demonstrating his command of seamanship by avoiding the windward side of the island, now appropriately named the Bay of Wrecks. Cook had a habit of naming islands for whatever holiday coincided with his visit. It is probably fortunate for geographers and postal services that he spent two of his exploratory yuletides bobbing around in the empty Antarctic. As it is, he left us only one other Christmas Island, and that one is conveniently located an ocean away, south of Java.

And so Cook gave the island a new name, took several hundred turtles in return, and left unimpressed, as recorded in his journal entry of January 2, 1778, the day of his departure:

There were not the smallest traces of any human being having ever been here before us; and indeed, should anyone be so unfortunate as to be accidentally driven upon the island, or left there, it is hard to say, that he could be able to prolong existence.

For the next century and a half, control of the island bounced around among the various colonial influences playing checkers with the islands of the mid-Pacific, including the British Crown, the American State Department, and a lunatic French priest named Petrics Rougier. The island's geopolitical importance rose and fell with the world's demand for fertilizer, copra, and mother-of-pearl buttons. In decidedly unclerical fashion, Rougier more or less owned the island outright for several decades after the turn of this century. During this time, he imported laborers from nearby islands to work on his coconut plantations. While he rewarded these poor people with nothing more than various combinations of religion and abuse, Rougier's laborers formed the nucleus of the island's first permanent population.

During the Second World War, American soldiers landed on the island, built an airfield, and defended it against a Japanese attack that never came. Ten years later, the British decided that they owned the island after all. They expressed their enthusiasm for the place by touching off a series of hydrogen bombs, after assuring the locals that this was all basically just a lot of harmless fun. Then we all left and gave the island back to the Gilbertese.

I have always been amazed by the Gilbertese people's willingness to have anything to do with us, since virtually the only things our culture has brought to Christmas Island are Coca-Cola, nuclear fallout, and conflict. My first impression of the island's natives was that they were the most genuinely innocent people I had ever met. They seemed constitutionally incapable of argument. We wasted no time in showing them how it is done.

The first afternoon we spent on the island, Ray and I piled into a truck with a native driver and a well-heeled older couple and set off to look for bonefish. This took place in the early days of the island's development as a fly-fishing destination, and nobody knew what the hell they were doing, especially us. We drove through a warren of rough roads and scrub brush in back of the island's vast lagoon, until our driver finally pulled over, smiled, and pointed to the sea. That was plenty good enough for Ray and me, although our accidental companions were plainly put off by all the confusion, the lack of English-speaking guides, and a long list of related complaints which they did not hesitate to share with us. "Aw, screw 'em," Ray whispered tactfully as we readied our gear. "Let's go fishing." Which we did.

There were only a couple of hours of light left, and we wanted to cover some water and do as much exploring as possible. Ray went one way and I went another, leaving the older couple to grumble their way in little circles around the truck. Screw 'em is right, I thought, as I slogged through the ankle-deep water in search of my first Pacific bone. I mean, come *on*.

As it turned out, there were bonefish all over the place, as there usually are nearly everywhere you go on Christmas Island. I spent an hour learning an important local lesson, which is that one should ignore bonefish sulking around in quiet water and work the windward points where the fish are more likely to be active. Finally I stumbled into a cut between two coral heads, where the wind was pushing the water past phalanxes of eager bonefish, and I caught them one after another until I ran out of light.

I returned to the truck to find Ray MIA, our driver looking pleasantly befuddled, and our two compatriots more than a little out of sorts. He made a point of studying his watch. She stared at me just the way my mother used to stare when I was late for dinner. "Wanna beer?" I asked, since I had filled the ice chest in the back of the truck with survival fare prior to our departure from the hotel.

"No, thank you," she replied, in a voice that could rotenone a lake.

"Catch some fish?" I went on, as I popped the top off one for myself.

"What we've been doing," he said, "is waiting. For you and your friend."

"For quite some time now," she pointed out. "We're anxious to get back and freshen up."

"Ray was right," I muttered under my breath. The truck was becoming intolerable. I walked down toward the water and tried to strike up a conversation with our driver. He was shy and spoke almost no English, but we somehow managed to pantomime our way to a series of agreements: Fishing was fun, cold beer was good, and the two people sitting in the back of the truck were dick-heads. Or something like that.

He was obviously dismayed by the dissension in the air. It was my honest opinion that he had never witnessed a dispute before, much less been a participant in one. He sure as hell was now. By the time Ray slogged out of the gloom with tales of bonefish by the hundred, the couple in the back of the truck weren't even speaking to each other, let alone either of us. We climbed up front with the driver and the rest of the beer, and by the time we got back to the hotel Ray had a nickname—All Day Ray—that followed him through half a dozen subsequent trips to Christmas, to the delight of the more enthusiastic guides and the dismay of their lazier brethren. The couple in the back of the truck managed to spend the next ten days on the island without speaking to anyone in our party. They made it plain to everyone else at the hotel that we were deranged louts who cared more about bonefish and beer than the feelings of their fellow Americans, an opinion we would have endorsed heartily had there been an opportunity to do so.

Fortunately, we were too busy fishing.

Christmas Island has a reputation for small bonefish, a reputation that is accurate in a lopsided kind of way. Yes, there are a lot of small bonefish there. However, there are a lot of large bonefish as well, which serves to emphasize that these two conditions are not mutually exclusive.

I have never landed a double-digit bonefish on Christmas Island, but I have taken quite a few that were close. I also saw the second largest bonefish I have ever seen in my life there, and the memory of that fish alone is enough to dispel forever the small-fish rap on Christmas Island.

This encounter came early one afternoon when I was exploring new water, and as so often seems the case with truly big bones, the fish was behaving atypically. I was way out in the middle of nowhere after a morning of swimming and hiking through the lagoon, and it was quite possible that no sport angler had ever fished this flat before. I had just taken a couple of fish in the five-pound range and seen some larger ones out near the edge of the blue water. The wind was kicking up spray as I walked along a coral shelf in search of a comfortable place to sit down and eat a bite of lunch.

Suddenly, a shadow appeared right out from under the shelf in front of me, only to disappear back below the overhang again. I stopped and stared at what seemed at first to have been a mirage, but then I could see the shape of a fish finning slowly beneath the coral. It wasn't moving, and what little of it I could see didn't look much like a bonefish.

But, as I learned long ago: When in doubt, cast! I did, and the mysterious shape detached itself from the coral, feinted in the direction of my fly, then retreated toward the deep water like a grumpy old man awakened from a nap. The fish was so big that it took a moment to realize what it was. Then, before it vanished into the channel's blue haze, we made eye contact briefly, as if the fish meant to address me personally, which is ludicrous, except that this romantic notion gives me a marvelous excuse to think about going back again and again.

How big was that bonefish? Fifteen pounds easily, and perhaps one or two more. I'm no enthusiast of weights and measures in outdoor sport, and this approximation will just have to do, especially since I didn't catch the fish. But you get a good idea. It was big enough so that I'll never have to listen to people complain about Christmas Island's small bonefish again unless I want to.

I made half a dozen trips to Christmas Island in the 1980s, the early years of its development as an obligatory stop on the light-tackle saltwater circuit. I kept going back both because the fishing was good and because

I lived in Alaska then, and Christmas was a readily accessible destination when cold and darkness held us hostage back at home. During those years, the fishing actually got better, as I learned the water and the peculiarities of the place, which always managed to feel different from traditional Caribbean bonefish venues even though the fish themselves looked just the same.

The ambience of the island itself, however, changed profoundly. In the early years, the island's residents were perhaps the most socially uncorrupted people I had ever known. As noted earlier, they had no historical reason to like us or even to tolerate our presence on their island, but they did. The language barrier made getting to know them difficult, but we managed anyway, and doing so allowed a glimpse of what it might be like to live free of the culturally sanctioned imperative to acquire and possess. I admit that verdict contains an ample dose of western naïveté in the spirit of Margaret Mead and Paul Gauguin, but the impulse is genuine and not altogether inaccurate.

And the great bumbling inefficiency of the place back then contributed in no small measure to its charm. The guides didn't know what the hell we wanted, so we got to learn the water together, a shortcoming that made me fall in love with the place the way you always love places more when you earn their favors for yourself. Of course, not everyone saw it that way, as we found out our very first day on the island, but that was their problem.

I admit that the Keystone Cops atmosphere sometimes became a little too much even for us. There was the time when Sheli and I staggered off the Anchorage-to-Honolulu redeye in our winter woolens only to learn that Air Tungaru, the charmingly inefficient airline that provides flight service from Hawaii to Christmas Island, had sold their one and only jet that week, leaving us no way to get where we were supposed to be going. That news led to an uncharacteristic rampage of ass-chewing on my part, after which it is remarkable that I was ever allowed anywhere near Christmas Island again, although everyone forgave everyone else in the end.

It couldn't last and it didn't. Each year the operation grew a little more crisp and efficient. Local guides were replaced by off-islanders from Tarawa who wore wristwatches and knew how to use them. A military ambience crept into the morning roll call at the Captain Cook Hotel, with charts and maps so that anglers could actually discuss (and argue about) who would be fishing where. Locals stopped giggling about money, and finally let it be known that they wouldn't mind having a little more of it themselves. Finally it became clear that going fishing on Christmas Island had become just what it has become wherever people with time and means choose to make it so: a business. Kiritimati would never be the same.

Economic determinists will not be surprised to see bonefish become another commodity in the end, as capable of inducing corruption as guano or copra or mother-of-pearl. Some may choose to frame this inflow of fishing dollars in terms of Third World empowerment, which is a reasonable enough argument, except that about all I've seen money bring to the island is bad music, soft-drink cans, and anxiety. It doesn't matter now anyway, because the genie is out of the bottle and it isn't going back in under any circumstances imaginable. It never does.

As the island became more familiar and less extraordinary, I began exploring new saltwater destinations. It wasn't that there was anything wrong with the fishing at Christmas Island. On the contrary, I understand that it is every bit as good as it ever was. I just miss the dreamy quality of the place as we once knew it, and hate to confront my own share of responsibility for the loss of innocence that occurred.

Instead, I'll take the memories, of the night the water sprouted bonefish tails like weeds, and of the look the big one gave me as it teased my imagination relentlessly out to sea.